BIRDS

Greater Spotted Woodpecker (Dendrocopos major)

BIRDS

igloobooks

igl00books

Published in 2014
by Igloo Books Ltd,
Cottage Farm,
Sywell
NN6 0BJ
www.igloobooks.com

LEO002 0414
2 4 6 8 10 9 7 5 3 1
ISBN: 978-1-78343-482-4

Printed and manufactured in China

*A Sparrowhawk on the trunk of a felled
pine – their broad, rounded wings and
long tail are adapted for flying between
trees and branches, enabling them to
weave in and out of trees at high speed.*

CONTENTS

A MESSAGE FROM
NIGEL BLAKE
BIRD PHOTOGRAPHER

I have been photographing birds for over thirty years, as both amateur and professional. It has been a most absorbing, interesting and all-encompassing hobby, and still fills me with delight. When I began, my initial failure to get good shots of birds taught me that what I needed in order to improve was to know more about them, their habits, histories and 'personalities'.

What makes a great bird photo? Well, we all have a different eye as to what makes a great shot. All I can do is show you what I can see and sometimes capture. While I may use some some of the best cameras and lenses available, I am sure it is not just about equipment, just as owning a top brand of clubs will not ensure that you can shoot a sub-par round of golf. It's also not just about technical details such as sharpness, or 'depth of field', or composition techniques. For me it is truly about developing a sensitive and understanding relationship with the other life forms with whom we share this planet.

Digital cameras have now become good enough and inexpensive enough for almost anyone to enjoy bird photography, but whether you photograph birds or merely observe them there are two things I would earnestly recommend.

First, realise that nature is not something that only occurs many miles away in exotic locations – it is all around us and we are in constant interaction with it. A surprisingly large proportion of my best images are taken close to home.

Second, and I cannot stress this point too strongly, is that I want all bird photographers to enjoy their craft responsibly and with the utmost respect for their subjects – if birds are getting stressed by your presence or actions, back off and don't take the shot!

INTRODUCTION

Birds have a special place in our affections. Their song adds a cheery note to our everyday life; and the sight of any one of our five hundred or more species gladdens our hearts. Birds put us in touch with the natural world, reminding us that we share this planet with other creatures whose needs we must respect. This book will introduce you to some of the many birds you can see, and help you to get to know them better.

A nightingale sings its heart out.

The Dawn Chorus

In its simple way the dawn chorus is one of the wonders of the countryside. At the first glow of the rising sun birds begin to sing, with more joining the 'orchestra' as night turns to day until the volume and variety of sounds becomes astounding.

It is at its best in early May and the experience more than repays the effort it takes to get yourself out of your bed in time to hear it. To its human audience the dawn chorus sounds like a celebration of the season and of better days to come – to hear it is an uplifting experience.

Of course, that interpretation sees bird behavior through the distorting lens of human feelings. In reality birdsong is a practical thing – it is about attracting a mate and communicating ownership of territory. But it would be wrong to completely detach the biology of birds from of our feelings for them. A world without birdsong would be a poorer place.

That cheerless vision caught the imagination of the public in the United States – and later the wider world – in the early 1960s following the publication of Rachel Carson's book *Silent Spring*, which is credited with being a major impetus for the environmental movement that has so influenced the way we live today. The book was a response to her growing concern about the indiscriminate use of the pesticide DDT and it painted a picture of American communities in which all life is silenced by the slow, insidious damage done by pesticide use.

Carson said her work was prompted by the experience of a friend who had seen birds die as a result of the aerial DDT spraying around her home to control mosquitoes. It also looked at more insidious damage done by uncontrolled pesticide use, such as the way pesticides thinned the shells of birds' eggs, leading to breeding failure. The prospect of a world in which the birds have been silenced struck such a chord with the public that an official investigation into DDT's impact on the environment was commissioned. In 1972 DDT use was banned in the US; other countries followed suit, including the UK. Today, fortunately, we do not have to hear a silent spring. The dawn chorus is still with us.

Blackbirds are one of the most recognisable of our garden birds.

Birds and folklore

Birds undoubtedly have a special place in our affections, and they have done for many generations. Generally, our ancestors had a more practical, utilitarian attitude to the natural world than we do today. But the wealth of bird-related folklore that has come down to us suggests they were moved by the colour, beauty, magic and even menace of birds. One Somerset tradition warned that a baby would die if eggs were stolen from a Raven's nest.

In many cultures the behaviour of birds was said to offer up clues to what the future might hold. For example, in ancient Rome priests known as augurs interpreted the will of the gods by studying the natural world. The flight of the birds was thought to be especially meaningful and an augur would see significance from details such as direction of flight, whether or not birds called in flight and whether they flew alone or flocked together. Something of this sense that birds bring omens stays with us today. For example, in most parts of the country a gathering of Magpies is seen as an indicator of good or bad fortune depending on how many birds are seen at any one time, and most people know a few lines of one version of the rhyme which begins:

One for sorrow, two for mirth,
Three for a wedding, four for a birth.

With its noisy chattering, black-and-white plumage and long tail, there is nothing else quite like the Magpie.

The importance of territory

Birds lead very varied lives. Evolution has adapted bird species to exploit just about every available habitat and, from Avocet to Tawny Owl, their diversity is incredible. However, species do share common features. Song and territory is one shared feature, with many birds staking a claim, through song, to a breeding territory that they will then defend against others of the same species.

Species that live in habitats where visibility is poor often have the most powerful singing voices. For instance a Sedge Warbler has a loud song that carries over a long distance to warn other Warblers that its section of reed bed is taken.

A good territory can be vital to breeding success. As bird parents raise their hungry families they rely on their surrounding territory to offer up a reliable supply of food for their youngsters. If there is plenty of food close to the nest then a pair clearly has an advantage.

Other species take a different approach by breeding in colonies – this includes Rooks, Herons and many seabirds such as Puffins and Gannets. In a colony there is a degree of shared security and birds foraging for food together can also gain advantages.

Producing young

The vast majority of the UK's two hundred or so breeding species lay their eggs in some sort of nest although the level of complexity involved in construction varies widely. The nest of the Song Thrush involves hours of work to put together. First the female weaves twigs and dried grass into a deep, cup-shaped bowl in a well-covered position in a tree or bush. She then lines the cup with beakfuls of mud, which dry to form a sturdy base for her clutch of eggs.

A quite different tack is taken by the Lapwing, which takes a more minimalist approach, laying its eggs in a shallow scrape out in the open, in a ploughed field or on grassland. Its speckled eggs are well camouflaged against a sparse mat of grass or other vegetation.

Two very different types of nestling hatch in these two contrasting nests, according to the safety or otherwise of their environment. Thrush chicks are classed as nidicolous, or nest-attached, which means they come into the world helpless and without feathers. They need constant care from their parents and two weeks have to pass before they are ready to leave the nest. Lapwing chicks are nidifugous and leave the nest on their first day. They have feathers when they hatch and are able to run within hours, but do not fly until they are a month old. They are fed by their parents, who will also defend them against predators as far as they can.

All-black and larger than its cousin the Moorhen, the Coot has a distinctive white beak and 'shield' above the beak.

Wild birds can be surprisingly long-lived, but average lifespans are far shorter. So, the average life expectancy for a Tawny Owl is just five years, but there are plenty of records of wild owls aged over 20 and even of a 21-year-old Tawny Owl mother. The mismatch between record ages and averages is a result of some fairly grim mathematics; the fact is that for many species the odds are stacked against young birds.

One example is the Swallow, which can have three broods of young in a single season. That means that an adult pair could produce between 12 and 15 young in a single summer. Of those dozen young Swallows only one or two are likely to survive their first year. The first months of independent life involve a steep learning curve, but once a bird has learned the art of survival its chances of living to a ripe old age are excellent.

Blackbird eggs are a distinctive blue, while those of the Little Tern make them almost invisible in their sandy scrapes.

Built for purpose

Most birds fly, and their bodies have evolved to meet the requirements of flight. The bones of their fore limbs are long and have a honeycomb structure to minimize their weight.

From their 'wrist' joint they have two finger bones and a thumb. It is the finger bones that carry the primary feathers, which cut through the air as a bird flies. The wings are braced by the wishbone and the wing muscles are firmly anchored to a big breastbone.

But while there is some uniformity in wing structure, much of the rest of a bird's body shape is geared to its special role in its ecosystem. Eye shape and position on the head, leg shape and beak shape are all incredibly varied and their form is often dictated by a particular function.

It is a variety that can be seen clearly if you spend some time watching birds feeding below the high-tide mark on an estuary. This is a very rich environment and lots of birds visit to feed on the many small creatures that live in tidal mud and sand. Some, like the Curlew, have long, thin legs that allow them to wade through water and a long, thin bill that probes deep in wet mud for worms. In contrast the Shelduck has shorter legs and a short, splayed bill which it uses to search through mud close to the surface for small shellfish.

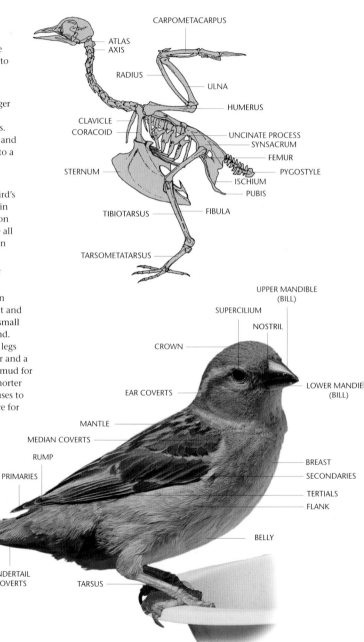

CARPOMETACARPUS
ATLAS
AXIS
RADIUS
ULNA
HUMERUS
CLAVICLE
CORACOID
UNCINATE PROCESS
SYNSACRUM
FEMUR
PYGOSTYLE
STERNUM
ISCHIUM
PUBIS
TIBIOTARSUS
FIBULA
TARSOMETATARSUS

UPPER MANDIBLE (BILL)
SUPERCILIUM
NOSTRIL
CROWN
LOWER MANDIE (BILL)
EAR COVERTS
MANTLE
MEDIAN COVERTS
RUMP
BREAST
SECONDARIES
PRIMARIES
TERTIALS
FLANK
TAIL
BELLY
UNDERTAIL COVERTS
TARSUS

Eye shape and form also vary to fit purpose. The eyesight of birds is especially sharp, which is an advantage to both birds of prey and species that are themselves the prey of birds and animals.

Like us humans, birds of prey have eyes on the front of their heads. As a result the fields of vision of the two eyes overlap to create a wide arc of three-dimensional vision. Species that have to evade predators often have eyes on the sides of their head, which gives them poorer sight, but means that they can see what is happening all around them.

No creature can see in complete darkness, but Barn Owl eyes are twice as sensitive to low light as human eyes, helping them hunt at night.

Dinosaurs and birds

The most widely-held version of bird evolution starts around the end of the Jurassic period, more than 150 million years ago, with a feathered dinosaur, *Archaeopteryx lithographica*. The bird-like features of *Archaeopteryx* included feathers of the right shape and form for flight – however the function of those early feathers is the subject of ongoing debate. One argument is that feather-like structures first evolved for some purpose unrelated to flight (like display or insulation), but that incidentally they helped the animals to jump a little higher or a little further. That may have been a competitive advantage that over the millennia evolved into an ability to glide and, later, to fly. Recent discoveries have shown that some early feathers were probably colourful. Although we think of dinosaurs as being dull battleship grey, at least some may have had brightly-coloured plumage, possibly to attract the opposite sex.

Over further millennia, the more bird-like of these dinosaurs evolved into early birds, and those early birds are in turn the ancestors of the Robin on the garden bird table and all the other birds that we see around us today.

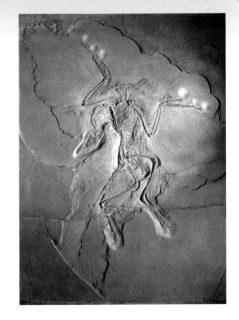

Archaeopteryx lithographica specimen displayed at the Museum für Naturkunde *in Berlin.*

Supreme skill

What birds have evolved to do with supreme skill is, of course, fly. Yet of a bird's feathers only a few are flight feathers, with the majority doing other jobs such as weatherproofing and insulation.

Flight feathers are stiff and long. They also have tiny hooks that bond them together so that they form a strong, light structure that can resist air. Add to these feathers a super-light body and the bird has much of what is required for flight. But in order to take to the air a creature must exert a burst of muscle-power; you only have to watch a Mute Swan fighting to get airborne to understand that lots of energy goes into getting a bird up and into the air. Once off the ground it takes relatively little energy to keep a bird on the move – as can be attested by those of us who have watched and admired the effortless flight of a Herring Gull.

The magnificent White-tailed Eagle is still a rare breeder following its extinction and reintroduction.

Different lifestyles demand different types of flight. Most garden birds are generalists – they need to be manoeuvrable, but little more. Other species though need something more specialized. The Red Kite is a majestic bird of prey which covers huge distances searching for food; to do so it uses an energy-light approach to flight that minimizes wing beats and takes best advantage of air movements.

The Peregrine Falcon has a quite different flying style. The Peregrine uses speed to overtake and bring down its prey, small birds. It can reach speeds of up to 129 km/hr (80 mph) in level flight, but it usually strikes prey from height in stooping dive that sees it fold back its wings to go into a near-vertical descent. In a dive the Peregrine has been shown to reach 322 km/hr (200 mph).

Identifying birds

Altogether more than 500 different birds rate as UK species, but only about a third of that number are resident here or are regular visitors. So for the novice, learning the basics should be relatively straightforward. This book will introduce you to the most commonly seen birds and some of those less commonly seen. In order to take the next step, a good identification guide is invaluable, but do choose your guide with care. Beginners often start out with a guide to the birds of the UK and Europe, which can be a problem because it introduces images and description of birds that you are highly unlikely to see on this side of the English Channel. As a result confusion sets in when it comes to making a good identification in the field.

It is a good idea to concentrate on getting to know the thirty or so commonest species – though in practice that means getting to know many more 'faces' because for many species the plumage of males and females are quite different. As a rule male birds have showier, more brightly coloured plumage to attract a mate, while females are drabber so they can blend into the background when sitting on eggs. However, this is not always the case – for example, male and female Robins are impossible to tell apart.

A further complication is that young birds often take a year or two to mature. In the case of the Herring Gull, the familiar gull typically seen in any seaside town, birds have mottled brown feathers for the first three years of life and only grow the familiar sleek white and pale grey plumage when they become sexually mature at four years of age.

All of this means you should not rely entirely on plumage as a clue to identification. Learning to recognize bird calls is just as useful, so a CD of bird calls and songs can be a wise investment. Just as useful can be a knowledge of bird behaviour. Over time you will learn to know what species do. So for example, when you see a small brown bird at a distance working its way over the bark of a tree trunk from base to boughs you will know that that behaviour makes it almost certainly a Treecreeper.

Eider, showing different colourations.
From top: immature male, young adult male, adult male and adult female

MIGRATION

It is widely known that the Cuckoo is a migrant; its first call in spring is a welcome reminder of the coming of summer. But how many of us are aware that the friendly Robin may have just arrived from Poland, or the noisy Starling may flown in from Russia? Find out more about which birds migrate, and why, in the next few pages.

Summer visitors

The Swift is very much a bird of high summer. On sultry August evenings small groups of the dark, scimitar-shaped birds fly circuits above village greens and city streets in what to our eyes can seem a celebration of flight.

However, although it is one of a number of species that are thought of as very much a feature of summer, the Swift actually spends just a few brief weeks here each year. Of all the bird species that come to the British Isles to breed during the summer it is the last to arrive and the first to leave.

Swifts end their long journey from their wintering grounds in southern Africa long after other summer arrivals like Swallows, House Martins and Cuckoos. The exact date of their arrival varies from year to year and from place to place, but most years they turn up at nesting sites around the end of April or beginning of May. Once here they stay just four months before heading south once again, to catch the rainy season south of the Equator. For so a small creature to undertake so long and perilous a journey for such a short stay does not seem to make sense.

So why do Swifts and all the other birds that come to the British Isles for the summer do it? The answer is simple – for food. In their wintering grounds insect-eating birds would face intense competition for food if they stayed put all year, so it pays to move to somewhere without that competition.

Visitors find a good supply of insect prey during our summer. There is also the advantage that our summer days are much longer than those of countries around the Equator, which is a boon to parent birds that have to work hard to feed their growing young.

Winter visitors

Migration is not only about birds that come here in spring and leave in autumn. Most of us know that some birds are resident, spending all year here, while others are migrants. Swifts, Swallows and Cuckoos are some of the best-known summer visitors, but there are other less well-known species that fly long distances to visit Britain at other times of year.

Some bird species head south in autumn to take advantage of what is a relatively mild, maritime climate compared with the long, hard winter they would experience if they remained in their breeding grounds. Lots of wetland species relocate in this way, coming to the open waters of our waterways, fens and estuaries. For example, Whooper Swans breed in the sub-Arctic, and those that spend their summer in Iceland overwinter in Scotland, Ireland, and parts of northern England.

The Swift is almost constantly on the wing.

Varied behaviour patterns

There are also some species that do not fit easily into the resident–migrant split. Many people who feed the birds in their garden feel a sense of ownership over their regular visitors, thinking of the Robin at the bird table or the Starling on the peanut feeder as neighbours. In fact, during the winter months there's a good chance the Robin may have arrived from the other side of Europe, while the Starling could have flown in from Russia. That's because many resident breeding populations of familiar species like Robin, Starling, Chaffinch and Blackbird are joined during the winter by incoming migrants of the same species. To us, the stay-at-home resident and the long-distance traveller look the same, but one will have covered hundreds, even thousands of miles to enjoy the advantages that come with winter here.

In many cases these winter in-migrations take place in some years but not in others – or not on the same scale. A lot depends on climate and food availability where the birds breed.

One example is our smallest bird, the Goldcrest. These tiny birds (an adult Goldcrest weighs around the same as a 20p piece) breed here, but during some winters many thousands more cross the North Sea to join them, in order to escape punishing temperatures in the conifer forests of Scandinavia and the Baltic states.

These incomers often arrive in October and November in large flocks. When they finally make landfall on the coast of England and Scotland the exhausted birds cannot go any further, and bushes and trees 'drip' with recovering Goldcrests. After getting over their journey the birds move on, some heading west into the rest of Britain and Ireland, others moving on to Europe.

Ringing birds to track movement

Another aspect of all this moving around is that some species make short-hop migrations within the British Isles. The practice of ringing birds allows scientists to collect data that tells us a great deal about the journeys birds undertake, including mini-migrations that might otherwise go unnoticed. Ringing involves attaching small metal rings to the legs of birds, either when they are in the nest or when they are caught in nets set up for the purpose. As each ring carries a unique code the wearer's movements can be mapped when they are later recaptured or found dead.

The process provides researchers with useful evidence about migration routes. More about the marathon trips later; first an example of migration on a modest scale. A few years ago a bird ringer in Norfolk put rings on a garden blackbird fresh out of the nest and that winter the bird was seen in a Devon garden, where it was a regular visitor. It arrived in December and left in mid-February. Over subsequent years it turned out that this otherwise rather ordinary bird lived something of a double life. Year in, year out, it followed the same routine, dividing its time between the same two gardens 230 miles (365km) apart.

Goldcrests migrate enormous distances for such a tiny bird.

Changing habits

A final aspect of all this mobility is that migration habits can and do change. One example is the Blackcap, a small, grey-brown warbler with a powerful and tuneful song. Half a century ago it was possible to say that the Blackcap was a summer visitor that migrated to the Iberian Peninsula and North Africa for the winter months, returning in March and April to breed. More recently a growing number of garden birders have reported Blackcaps feeding at winter bird tables. At first the assumption was that these birds were summer visitors that were choosing to stay put due to milder winters. However, further study has shown that the picture is a little more complicated; winter Blackcaps appear to be birds that breed in central Europe that are now flying west in autumn rather than heading south.

As with so many recent discoveries about bird migration, we owe our understanding of the changing habits of Europe's Blackcaps to the ongoing ringing effort. During just over a century of ringing, analysis of the data collected has transformed our understanding of the lives of birds. For the eighteenth-century naturalist Gilbert White the comings and goings of what he called birds of passage were a perplexing puzzle. His contemporaries believed that Swallows spent the winter in the mud below lakes and ponds, and although he searched, White could never find the sleeping birds.

Record-breaking travellers

Thanks to ringing we now know that Swallows that first see the light of day in nests in our barns spend the winter months in South Africa. Their long-haul journey follows a flyway that takes them over France and Spain, into north Africa, across the Sahara and the Gulf of Guinea, to the southern tip of the continent.

It is quite a distance, but the Swallow's migration feat is easily outstripped by the UK's long-haul voyager, the Arctic Tern. The sleek, fast-flying seabird – which is sometimes called the Sea Swallow – enjoys two summers each year, breeding in the Arctic and surrounding regions of the Northern Hemisphere and then flying 12,000 miles (19,000km) south to the Antarctic for the rest of the year.

Amazingly, in an average lifetime an Arctic Tern will fly close to 1.4m miles (2.3m km). Or perhaps the truly amazing aspect of bird migration is that birds navigate their way over such long distances so effortlessly.

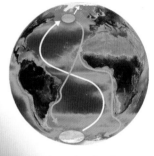

This map shows the migration pattern of the Arctic tern, from its breeding sites around the north Atlantic to the winter grounds in Antarctica.

Arctic Tern with its distinctive red bill.

How do birds know where to go?

Thanks to its breeding strategy of laying its eggs in the nest of other birds, the Cuckoo does not have to linger overlong in this country. By late June or early July the adults return to their wintering grounds, which are thought to be in east Africa.

Young Cuckoos leave their foster nests long after their natural parents have left Europe and have to find their own way south. How do they do it? It remains something of a mystery and is the subject of on-going research, but the best guess is that there is probably no single 'compass' that guides a migrating bird. It is more likely that a number of skills and senses combine to guide them on their way. Firstly, migrating birds are thought to use markers in the landscape to guide them over land or over the sea when in sight of land. There is evidence that man-made features like roads and railways are used.

Seasoned veterans probably lead the way, which means young birds can rely on their experience. However, many young birds – those young Cuckoos – have to travel alone, and recognizing landscape features cannot be of help to them. So it is most likely that birds have innate abilities that we struggle to understand. The sun and stars almost certainly play a part – in experiments, star patterns simulated with bulbs have been shown to influence decisions birds make about flight direction.

Finally, there is growing evidence that birds can read the Earth's magnetic field. It is hard to imagine how a bird could 'see' something that is hidden from us humans, but however it happens it is probably this inborn ability that guides young Cuckoos, Swifts and Swallows on their epic journeys.

TOWN AND GARDEN BIRDS

*Gardens, whether in town or country, usually provide abundant
food and shelter, which makes them excellent places to see a wide
range of birds – from the tiny Wren to the large Crow, from the dull
Dunnock to the colourful Goldfinch. Even the most built-up urban
environment has its advantages for some birds, with high ledges
away from predators and plenty of edible rubbish in the streets. Keep
your eyes open, and if you are lucky you will see most of the birds
described in this section.*

THE TOWN AND GARDEN HABITAT

As their natural habitats have become changed or destroyed through redevelopment, pollution and farming, towns and gardens have become a major source of food and shelter for birds. Even in their natural environment, birds are very adaptive: when there's a food shortage, they are able to respond by altering diet, or by relocating to areas where food sources are more plentiful. Once they find a good source of food, many birds can become sedentary, so it's hardly surprising that many species have adapted easily to city life and suburban gardens, where they find micro-habitats which mirror their natural environment.

It isn't only the quest for food that has encouraged this move. In winter, it's the search for warmth and shelter too. Just as non-migratory birds, such as finches, will sometimes travel south to warmer regions in winter, so birds can move into towns and cities, which are warmer than the surrounding countryside.

In the suburbs

Suburban gardens are attractive to birds, as many have been landscaped in such a way that they mimic the birds' natural habitats. Such gardens can often sustain a large number of different species in a relatively small area.

In the wild, many small birds, such as passerines (perching birds), are commonly found in hedgerows. These birds are happy to relocate to suburban hedges and shrubberies, while corvids (varieties of Crow) will nest in larger trees and forage in lawns.

Blue Tits and Great Tits willingly use bird boxes for nesting, and House Sparrows and Martins will sometimes do so. Sadly, the Sparrow is now on the decline, perhaps because changes in house design provide fewer of the nooks and crannies it used to like for nest-building, or maybe because of the birds of prey that occasionally venture into towns and suburbs.

There is further bad news. Due to the decline in traditional game-keeping, the number of Magpies has soared over the last 20 years, so much so that they have become pests in towns and gardens, as well as the countryside. These highly intelligent birds are capable of adapting their diet to almost any environment. In gardens, they will steal eggs and kill other young birds.

Food for the birds

But there is good news too. Gardens offer a wide variety of food for birds, and many birds are responding to this. Gardens that are dug regularly offer a readily available supply of worms, grubs and insects. Finches will visit gardens in early spring to take advantage of new growth in berry plants, and in the autumn and winter they relish seed heads which kind-hearted gardeners leave – resisting the temptation to tidy them away.

Ornamental ponds are an important part of many people's gardens, and suit birds too. They provide a crucial source of water for all species and can attract Swallows and Swifts, which relish the insect life associated with water.

Birds find plenty to eat even without the help of humans. But increasingly, people are putting out bird feeders of various kinds. There has been a noted rise in the number of Goldfinches, which have adapted their diet to include the sunflower seeds which are included in many seed mixes. Long-tailed Tits have recently made it into the list of top ten garden visitors. It is thought that the main reason is that people are providing a more varied diet in feeders than they have in the past.

Birds make use of garden opportunities in less conventional ways too, taking food or water from pet bowls and pilfering from picnics and barbecues.

Life in the city

Feral Pigeons have long been the mainstay of city centres, but now their numbers are on the wane as they compete for food with other species moving in from the countryside. Pigeons are also under attack from Peregrine Falcons, which are increasingly breeding on tall buildings. This once endangered bird of prey is making a comeback due to conservation measures, and has found a plentiful food source within our city centres.

The Starling has also acclimatized well to city life. Traditionally a mimic of other birds, Starlings now impersonate man-made sounds, such as cars and doorbells, to such an extent that it is getting more and more difficult to identify their natural call. Interestingly, although Starlings will eat just about any food we humans throw away, they will only feed invertebrates to their young.

Other common visitors include scavengers of the crow family such as Jackdaws and Magpies, which can often be seen clearing up the food refuse left at weekends by revellers. Magpies have also adapted well, feeding on roadkill while avoiding becoming roadkill themselves.

The evidence all points to one conclusion: as the natural environment of our countryside birds diminishes, most species find a way to adapt and successfully integrate into urban and suburban communities.

COMMON BLACKBIRD   *Turdus merula*

ADULT   The adult male Blackbird is easily recognizable due to its lustrous black plumage and orange-yellow bill. A ring of the same colour can be found around the eyes. An adult female is a dark brown-black with a dark yellow bill and subtle spotted underside. This is very similar to the markings of the Song Thrush, but darker and duller.

JUVENILE   The juvenile Blackbird varies between shades of dark and light brown, with darker birds usually being male. They too have dark bars or spots below: again, these markings always appear darker than those of the Song Thrush.

EGGS   Eggs are blue-green with deep red blotches. When fledged, the young will follow the parents from the nest in search of food. It is not uncommon for a female to then lay a new clutch, often in the same nest if the brood was successful. The male then assumes full responsibility for feeding the fledglings.

SONG   The Blackbird has a melodic, warbling song followed by a harsh, scratchy ending. They have various calls for aggression and defence, notably a high-pitched *seeee* when airborne predators are spotted, and a *pook pook* call for ground predators, which include cats and foxes.

DIET   The Blackbird is omnivorous, and eats a wide variety of foods such as insects, seeds and berries. They also sift through leaves and plants for earthworms, insects and grubs. Occasionally, small vertebrates such as frogs and lizards may be hunted.

LENGTH	23–29 cm (9–11½ in)
WINGSPAN	35–38 cm (14–15 in)
BREEDING STARTS	**March**
NUMBER OF EGGS PER CLUTCH	**3–5**

| J |
| F |
| M |
| A |
| M |
| J |
| J |
| A |
| S |
| O |
| N |
| D |

Where in UK Blackbirds can be seen

Months when Blackbirds can be seen

Female

Male

HABITAT   The Blackbird prefers gardens, parks and woodland where dense undergrowth and deciduous trees are present. As a result, the population of Blackbirds in built-up, urban areas and open spaces alike is very small.

OTHER   Blackbirds are very territorial. Males defend their territory with a 'bow and run' display, or by fighting with intruders. Females are less likely to come into conflict; however if a competitor for a nesting site is encountered during the breeding season, fighting can occur. Blackbirds are monogamous, and usually remain in a pair as long as they both survive.

BLUE TIT *Cyanistes caeruleus*

ADULT The Blue Tit is brightly coloured with a blue cap, white face and black bib, and a black bar across the eyes. The wings and tail are blue, with a yellow-green back and a distinctive yellow breast. Males and females are very similar, but the male has a slightly brighter colouring. In both cases, the bill is black, and legs are a blueish grey.

JUVENILE In juveniles there is little variance between male and female, but the young can be distinguished from their parents: the juvenile's face appears more yellow, the black bib is missing and the blue cap not yet present.

EGGS The Blue Tit will often nest in a small hole in a tree or wall, but willingly uses nesting boxes. Blue Tits are also renowned for nesting in peculiar places such as letter boxes and pipes. Commonly used materials are moss, wool, hair and plant matter; the nest is lined with down and formed into a cup shape. Eggs are white with brown-red spots. Incubation lasts from 12 to 16 days. After hatching, the chicks are fed by both parents.

SONG The Blue Tit's song is instantly recognizable: a quick, thin *tsee-tsee-tsu-hu-hu-hu*, with a chirring *see-see-seedudr* alarm call for predators, which include grey squirrels and Great Spotted Woodpeckers. Blue Tits are very active, making frequent calls with a lot of wing and tail flicking.

LENGTH	10–12 cm (4–5 in)
WINGSPAN	17–20 cm (6½–8 in)
BREEDING STARTS	April
NUMBER OF EGGS PER CLUTCH	5–16

J	
F	
M	
A	
M	
J	
J	
A	
S	
O	
N	
D	

Where in UK Blue Tits can be seen

Months when Blue Tits can be seen

DIET The chicks hatch when green caterpillars are in abundance, providing a major food source for them and their parents. In spring, Blue Tits also feed on nectar, pollen and seeds and, as acknowledged by many grateful gardeners, the birds eat aphids and many garden pests. In autumn, berries are popular. In winter, they take any available high-energy foods, and willingly feed on items put out by humans such as suet, sunflower hearts and peanuts. They have been known to peck through the foil tops of milk bottles to feed on the cream.

HABITAT Blue Tits thrive in many different habitats. They do well in the country and also near human habitation. They are sociable and can be found in groups searching trees, plants and hedgerows for food.

OTHER Blue Tits form flocks with other tit species in winter when food is scarce. They are incredibly agile, and it can be very entertaining to watch them feed from trees and hanging feeders.

CHAFFINCH   *Fringilla coelebs*

ADULT   The Chaffinch is one of the most colourful finches, and the male's striking orange-pink face and breast makes it one of the most recognizable garden birds. The summer male has a brown nape, green rump and a blue cap and tail, but this blue becomes chestnut brown in winter. The female is similar, but has an olive-brown breast and face year-round. The female is sometimes mistaken for the House Sparrow, but can be distinguished by her slimmer frame and white wing bars. The wings in both sexes are brown with white bars.

JUVENILE   The juveniles of both sexes are very like the adult female, but lack a green rump and appear almost white on the underside. The bill is brown in adult females and juveniles, and blue in adult males.

EGGS   Chaffinches tend to nest in tree forks, building a nest of moss or lichen, materials which act as camouflage. Eggs are green-blue with purple speckles. The female incubates them on her own for 10 to 16 days, but both parents are involved with feeding.

SONG   The Chaffinch is famed for its singing ability, with the male song sounding like *chip chip chooee, chooee.* It is also makes a *pink pink* call.

LENGTH	14–16 cm (5½–6½ ins)
WINGSPAN	25–29 cm (10–11½ ins)
BREEDING STARTS	April
NUMBER OF EGGS PER CLUTCH	2–8

Where in UK
Chaffinches
can be seen

Months when
Chaffinches
can be seen

DIET   The adults feed their young on insects, while also taking some of these for themselves. Juveniles and adults also eat caterpillars and seeds. You can often spot a Chaffinch sifting through leaf litter and under hedges for insects, or foraging for seeds beneath hanging feeders.

HABITAT   Chaffinches can be found in many different haunts. They do well in the country and the suburbs but less well in towns. They never travel far, most remaining within five miles of the place they were hatched. However, Chaffinches living on high ground may seek lower ground during winter.

OTHER   Chaffinches are territorial birds and defend both their territory and their personal space. Territorial defence is usually observed during the breeding season, whilst defence of personal space is most noticeable during winter when competition for food is high.

COLLARED DOVE   *Streptopelia decaocto*

ADULT   The Eurasian Collared Dove (commonly known as the Collared Dove) has a thin, black collar around the back of its neck. There are only minor differences between males and females: both are sandy grey-brown across the breast, wings and back, and have dark brown primary feathers which are visible at rest. The bill is slender and dark, and both sexes have red eyes. The head of the male is a light pinkish grey, whereas the female has a more orange-brown colouring.

JUVENILE   Juveniles have duller colours than adults and lack the black collar.

EGGS   Collared Doves nest on platforms made of sticks or twigs, in trees, or sometimes on buildings. These structures often appear remarkably flimsy and unable to support the weight of these large birds. The eggs are white and oval shaped. Both parents share incubation and feeding duties, although females tend to incubate at night and males during the day. It is common for the male to continue to feed fledglings whilst the female lays a second clutch.

SONG   The song of the Collared Dove is a distinctive *coo-COOO-coo*, often repeated many times. A loud *kwarr* is usually heard upon landing. Its song resembles the Latin word for the number 18, decaocto, to which the bird owes its name.

LENGTH	31–33 cm (12½–13 in)
WINGSPAN	47–55 cm (18½–21½ in)
BREEDING STARTS	March–Oct
NUMBER OF EGGS PER CLUTCH	2

Where in UK Collared Doves can be seen

Months when Collared Doves can be seen

DIET   Collared Doves mainly eat seeds, shoots and insects.

HABITAT   The Collared Dove is most common around human habitation, and can often be spotted on open lawns searching for food. It is a sedentary bird and will usually remain near the place where it was hatched. If it does travel, it will probably move west – a major reason for the rapid spread of the Collared Dove across Europe and into Britain, where there was no recorded population before 1955.

OTHER   The mating ritual, as with other pigeon species, consists of a rapid, near-vertical ascent followed by a long, circular glide downwards.

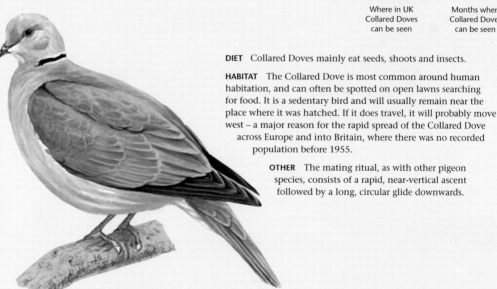

CARRION CROW *Corvus corone*

ADULT The Carrion Crow (usually simply called the Crow) is a large, flat-headed bird with a strong, black bill. It is entirely black at all ages, in all seasons. The Carrion Crow looks very like other species of crow, notably the Raven and the Rook. However the Crow's tail is less square than that of the Raven, and its plumage is tidier looking than a Rook's, especially at the top of the legs. Also, compared to a Rook, the bill is thicker and less pointed, and the flight pattern has more regular wingbeats and less gliding. The Carrion Crow was for many years considered to be the same species as the Hooded Crow, though they look very different. They are now known to be different species, though the two do interbreed.

JUVENILE The juvenile looks just like the adult.

EGGS The Carrion Crow nests high up, in the forks of trees, on cliff edges or even on electricity pylons. The nests are very large, made from sticks and lined with hair and bark. Both male and female build the nest and feed the young, but only the female incubates the eggs. These are a pale blue-green with dark brown and grey markings. Incubation lasts around 18 to 20 days.

SONG The call of the Carrion Crow is a harsh croak: *craarr, craarr, craarr.*

DIET Crows eat a wide range of food including worms, insects, fruit and seeds. They also eat eggs and young birds, and so are often persecuted in the countryside by gamekeepers who view the bird as a pest.

LENGTH	45–50 cm (18–19½ in)
WINGSPAN	95–104 cm (37½–50 in)
BREEDING STARTS	April
NUMBER OF EGGS PER CLUTCH	4–7

Where in UK Carrion Crows can be seen

Months when Carrion Crows can be seen

Carrion Crow

Hooded Crow

HABITAT Carrion Crows are present throughout the British Isles. They can often be spotted perched high up, in a tree or, in urban areas, a television aerial or telegraph pole. This gives them an excellent vantage point from which to spot food.

OTHER Carrion Crows display signs of intelligence and, though wary of humans, they soon learn when an area is safe and quickly return to take advantage of any food sources. They have also been known to monitor other birds building nests, and remember their location so later on they can snatch chicks from the nest. In winter, crows join groups with other crows visiting from Europe. A group of crows is called a 'murder'.

GREENFINCH *Carduelis chloris*

ADULT The Greenfinch (once known also as the Green Linnet) is a colourful garden visitor. The male is an olive-green in summer, with yellow tail and primary wing feathers. It has a broad body with a yellow rump, and the cheeks and tip of the tail are grey. During winter, the male retains the same plumage but appears duller. The female is grey-brown with a slight yellowing on the underside and breast. The tail and rump are more green-yellow, as are the wings. The stout bills and legs of both sexes are flesh coloured.

JUVENILE The juvenile Greenfinch of both sexes appears very similar to the adult female, only with darker streaks above and below. Juveniles can often be mistaken for House Sparrows.

EGGS Greenfinches nest in large numbers, usually together in a thicket or deep shrubs. Nests are made from twigs and grass, and lined with fine plant roots and hair. Eggs are beige, with black markings. They are incubated by the female for about 12 to 14 days. Both parents feed the hatchlings, and it is not uncommon for the female to lay another clutch or even two.

SONG The song of the Greenfinch is a wheezy *dweeeee*, whilst the call is a rapid *chitchitchitchit*, with a variety of rich trills at varying speed in between.

LENGTH	15 cm (6 in)
WINGSPAN	25–28 cm (10–11 in)
BREEDING STARTS	April
NUMBER OF EGGS PER CLUTCH	3–8

| J |
| F |
| M |
| A |
| M |
| J |
| J |
| A |
| S |
| O |
| N |
| D |

Where in UK Greenfinches can be seen

Months when Greenfinches can be seen

Female

Male

DIET Greenfinches usually eat seeds, insects, buds and berries. They are a common sight at hanging feeders, where they will eat sunflower seeds or peanuts, often clinging on for several minutes at a time to feed. If a seed mix is offered, they will throw other seeds away in order to get at the sunflower seeds.

HABITAT The Greenfinch inhabits gardens, parks and country hedgerows. It is an increasingly common sight in gardens as farming methods have deprived it of many of the weed seeds which it once relied on.

OTHER It is a sociable bird, and in the past whole flocks could be seen together on arable farms, feeding. But though sociable, it sometimes squabbles at bird tables and feeders.

GREAT TIT   *Parus major*

ADULT   The Great Tit is the largest of the common tits. Both sexes have a black cap, nape and throat, with white cheeks, and a black stripe running down the centre of a yellow breast. The back is yellow-green and the rump is blue-grey; there is a white bar on the wings. Males have longer bodies than females, their colours are more vibrant and the stripe down the breast is also broader than that of a female.

JUVENILE   Juveniles appear similar to the adult females, with yellowish cheeks.

EGGS   Great Tits will nest in boxes or in holes in trees and walls, laying smooth, glossy white eggs which are spotted with purple-red. The female incubates the eggs for roughly 13 or 14 days, with both parents feeding the hatchlings. Great Tits never roam far from the place where they were hatched.

SONG   The Great Tit is known for its large singing repertoire, including the familiar *tea-cher, tea-cher*. Its call can be confused with that of the Chaffinch, which makes a *chink-chink* sound. All calls are high and clean, but the alarm call is harsh and quick.

LENGTH	14 cm (5½ in)
WINGSPAN	22–25 cm (8½–10 in)
BREEDING STARTS	March
NUMBER OF EGGS PER CLUTCH	7–12

J
F
M
A
M
J
J
A
S
O
N
D

Where in UK
Great Tits
can be seen

Months when
Great Tits
can be seen

DIET   Usually insectivorous, Great Tits eat caterpillars and spiders but will also take seeds and berries. It is a common sight to see Great Tits feeding from hanging feeders or taking kitchen scraps from bird tables. They have also been seen following smaller Coal Tits to take advantage of their food supplies.

HABITAT   Great Tits have a wide range of habitats, including gardens and different kinds of countryside. They can often be seen scouring the garden for seeds or insects, or on bird tables and feeders.

OTHER   Like other species of tit, the Great Tit will join huge flocks in the winter to search for food. In the summer months, they often use their size to bully smaller tits and can be quite aggressive. Until the mid-twentieth century, the bird was called the Great Titmouse.

HOUSE MARTIN   *Delichon urbicum*

ADULT   The House Martin is a small bird with glossy blue-black head and back, and brown wings. The breast and underside are white, as well as the cheeks, chin and tail coverts. This colouring is present in both males and females. The tail has a band of white above and is forked, but there is no elongation as with the Swallow. The bird has tiny white feathers covering the legs and feet.

JUVENILE   Juveniles are similar to adults but have a brown cap, and the blue-black colour is duller.

EGGS   House Martins nest under the eaves of barns, houses and other buildings. They have even been known to nest in ship hulls. The nests are hollow cups made from mud, though sometimes they make use of artificial nesting boxes if provided. The eggs are smooth and white. Both males and females incubate the eggs for 13 to 19 days, and then share feeding responsibilities. There can sometimes be a second or third clutch, with the young of the first brood often returning to help their parents feed the new hatchlings.

SONG   The song of the House Martin is a high-pitched twittering, and they have a soft, chirruping *tsew, tsew* call.

LENGTH	12–15 cm (5–6 in)
WINGSPAN	25–29 cm (10–11½ in)
BREEDING STARTS	April–May
NUMBER OF EGGS PER CLUTCH	2–6

J
F
M
A
M
J
J
A
S
O
N
D

Where in UK
House Martins
can be seen

Months when
House Martins
can be seen

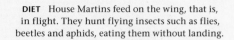

DIET   House Martins feed on the wing, that is, in flight. They hunt flying insects such as flies, beetles and aphids, eating them without landing.

HABITAT   They can be spotted flying in open spaces, searching for food, or collecting mud with which to build a nest. They tend to stay away from built-up areas, preferring locations with clean air. House Martins can also be seen in large colonies on telegraph lines and south-facing roofs. Just before settling to roost, you can see them flying erratically and at speed. They become very restless in autumn, just before they leave to spend the winter in Africa.

OTHER   House Martins return to the same place each year, flying thousands of miles to nest and reproduce in the same spot. They have been known to track hot air balloons, flying in circles above them. This is presumably to gain lift from the thermal stream produced.

HOUSE SPARROW   *Passer domesticus*

ADULT   Male House Sparrows have a chestnut brown back with black streaks, and a grey cap, rump and underside. They have a black bar across the eye, a white bar across the wing and a brown nape. They also have a black bib, the size of which reflects its status among other House Sparrows – the bigger the bib, the more dominant the bird. The bill is yellow-brown in summer and black in winter. The female is a paler brown and does not have the grey cap, black bib or eye bar. However, there is a straw-coloured band behind the eye, and a thinner white band on the wing.

JUVENILE   Juveniles appear similar to the adult female.

EGGS   House Sparrows live in large groups very near people, so they can be found nesting in holes or crevices in buildings or amongst creeping plants on houses. They build a cup-shaped nest from any material they can find. They also use nesting boxes if provided, and have been known to drive some species of tit from their nests. They lay white eggs with either dark grey or black speckles. Both male and female incubate the eggs for between 11 and 14 days; however the female spends more time carrying out this duty. Both adults feed the hatchlings. House Sparrows usually raise three clutches in a breeding season.

SONG   The House Sparrow's song is a cheerful-sounding chirruping and chirping which develops into a prolonged song.

DIET   House Sparrows have a very diverse diet and will eat seeds, nuts, berries, buds, insects and kitchen scraps. House Sparrows are often seen on bird tables and foraging in groups on the ground.

HABITAT   The House Sparrow is a noisy, cheerful bird which has declined in recent years but is still a familiar resident of towns and villages. Unlike the Tree Sparrow, its relative, it is less often seen in the countryside.

OTHER   In winter, House Sparrows often leave their groups in order to find food sources. There are many theories for the large decline of House Sparrows, including competition from the larger Collared Dove for food and the increasing number of cats as pets.

LENGTH	14–15 cm (5½–6 in)
WINGSPAN	21–25 cm (8–10 in)
BREEDING STARTS	May
NUMBER OF EGGS PER CLUTCH	3–5

Where in UK House Sparrows can be seen

Months when House Sparrows can be seen

J F M A M J J A S O N

Female

Male

MAGPIE   *Pica pica*

ADULT   The Common Magpie has an unmistakable appearance. At first glance, the adults have a black head, breast and nape, a white underside and steel blue wings, tail and rump. If you look closely, you will see that there are iridescent greens and purples amongst the tail feathers. The tail itself accounts for over half of the length of the Magpie, and is used as a status indicator within the species. Magpies often gather in large groups, with only breeding birds seeking solace.

JUVENILE   The juvenile Magpie is almost identical to the adult but lacks the length in the tail, and has a duller colouring. The bill of all sexes and ages is black, as are the legs.

EGGS   Both male and female construct the nest from twigs and sticks, which is then lined with mud and plant matter. Like other crows, nests are usually high in a large tree but can be found on electricity pylons. Magpie eggs are smooth and glossy, and pale blue in colour with brown or grey spots. The female will incubate the eggs for as long as 22 or 23 days.

SONG   The Magpie call is very distinctive: a harsh *chacker-chacker*.

LENGTH	44–46 cm (17–18 in)
WINGSPAN	52–60 cm (20½–23½ in)
BREEDING STARTS	April
NUMBER OF EGGS PER CLUTCH	5–8

Where in UK Magpies can be seen

Months when Magpies can be seen

DIET   They are omnivorous and will eat insects, carrion, grain, fruit, rodents and eggs. They also eat many types of kitchen scraps and can often be found scavenging in gardens and around human activity. They often prey on nestlings and fledglings of other species; however, they too are predated by the larger species of crow.

HABITAT   Magpies are resident in a wide variety of habitats, and are frequent garden visitors, although they are less common in upland and northerly districts. They are sedentary birds, and never roam far from their hatching place.

OTHER   As with other crows, the Common Magpie is highly intelligent and is one of few non-mammals to recognize itself in a mirror. Magpies are known to have an attraction to reflective and shiny objects, leading to a reputation as a thief. Often during the breeding season, a female Magpie can be distinguished from the male by having bent or damaged tail feathers.

ROBIN *Erithacus rubecula*

ADULT The Robin is a plump bird with a distinctive red breast and face and a white underside. Its head, wings, rump, tail, bill and legs are all brown. The male and female are almost indistinguishable, apart from the brown forehead which is 'V' shaped in females and a 'U' shape in males.

JUVENILE The juvenile Robin is brown all over, with speckled breast and underside. The juveniles lack the red breast of the adults so that they are not attacked over territorial disputes.

EGGS Robins have been known to nest in peculiar places including flowerpots, lawnmowers and car engines. A more usual nesting location is in a hole in a tree or wall, or in an open-fronted nesting box. The eggs are pale blue with red spots. The female incubates alone for around 12 to 15 days. The male will then help feed the young.

SONG The Robin's song is high-pitched and warbling. They can sometimes be heard at night in well-lit streets and this can lead to them being mistaken for the Nightingale. The alarm call is a sharp *tik tik*.

LENGTH	13–14 cm (5–5½ in)
WINGSPAN	20–22 cm (8–9 in)
BREEDING STARTS	March
NUMBER OF EGGS PER CLUTCH	3–9

Where in UK Robins can be seen

Months when Robins can be seen

DIET The diet is predominantly earthworms and insects. To find these items, they perch, watching the ground closely for any signs of movement. Robins also frequent tables and feeders, enjoying many sweet foods such as fruit cake and coconut cake as well as nuts. A very tame garden bird, they have been known to take mealworms from the hand.

HABITAT The Robin is widespread in town and country, although it is less common in Scotland. It is a popular garden visitor, especially in midwinter.

OTHER Robins are quite aggressive birds and do not tolerate intruders to their territory. They will often visit other territories during the breeding season to find a mate, which can lead to confrontation. They fight for food with other birds, especially tits, and have been known to completely drive away other species with similar diets.

SONG THRUSH   *Turdus philomelos*

ADULT Both male and female Song Thrushes are similar: plain brown on top with a pale yellow, speckled breast and an almost white underside. The markings on the breast are dark brown and linear. They are orange-yellow beneath the wings, with a similar colour bill and pink legs.

JUVENILE Juvenile Song Thrushes appear similar to the adults, but are a little lighter in colour.

EGGS The female builds her nest from grass, twigs and earth, usually in bushes and trees. In it she lays bright blue eggs with black spots, which she incubates herself for 11 to 15 days. Once hatched, the young are fed by both parents.

SONG As its name suggests, the Song Thrush is known for its melodic singing. It is common to hear the same song repeated three or four times. The alarm call is a swift *chook-chook-chook*.

DIET Thrushes are omnivorous and will eat snails, invertebrates, berries and fruit. As they are ground feeders, they rarely use bird tables or hanging feeders. Song Thrushes eat snails by using a stone as an anvil to crack open the shell. This trick is very useful when the ground has been baked by sun or frozen and they cannot reach earthworms.

LENGTH	23 cm (9 in)
WINGSPAN	33–36 cm (13–14 in)
BREEDING STARTS	March
NUMBER OF EGGS PER CLUTCH	3–9

Where in UK Song Thrushes can be seen

Months when Song Thrushes can be seen

HABITAT The Song Thrush is widespread throughout the country. It especially likes a mixture of open space and dense vegetation and is a common visitor to gardens. They are usually solitary birds, but it is not uncommon to see groups roosting together in winter or sharing feeding grounds.

OTHER Always alert, the Song Thrush adopts an upright posture when feeding, looking out for rival birds or predators, such as cats. As a result, Song Thrushes often feed close to the cover of hedgerows or bushes. They are easy to spot in the garden – when hunting earthworms, they stand cocking their head to the side and listening for movement below the ground. Song Thrushes can sometimes be seen on open lawns, where they will run or hop rapidly before stopping to survey the area, then moving along again.

STARLING   *Sturnus vulgaris*

ADULT The Starling is one of the noisiest and boldest garden birds. In summer, both sexes are a deep black with iridescent green and purple on the wings. This fades in winter as birds become lighter, with white spots on the head, breast and underside becoming more apparent. The male has fewer of these spots than the female. In both, the bill is pointed, turning from yellow in summer to brown in winter. The base of the beak is pink in females and blue in males.

JUVENILE Juveniles of both sexes are a mousey-brown colour with dark brown cheeks.

EGGS The male constructs the nest from grass, usually in a hole in a tree, wall or building. The female then lines the nest with feathers, wool and moss. Alternatively, they will use a medium-sized nesting box if available. Males often decorate the nest with leaves or petals in order to attract a mate. The female lays pale or light blue eggs, and both adults share incubation and feeding duties. It is common for a female Starling to remove an egg from another Starling's nest and replace it with one of her own to increase the survival rates of her own clutch.

SONG The Starling has a noisy, raucous song made up of a variety of squeaks, clicks and whistles. They have a talent for mimicry and have been known to imitate telephones and car alarms, as well as other birds.

LENGTH	**22 cm (8½ in)**
WINGSPAN	**37–42 cm (14½–17 in)**
BREEDING STARTS	**April**
NUMBER OF EGGS PER CLUTCH	**4–9**

Where in UK Starlings can be seen	Months when Starlings can be seen

DIET Starlings are not fussy eaters and will take invertebrates, berries, fruit and kitchen scraps. However, they only feed their young invertebrates such as earthworms and snails, as these provide the most nutrition. In gardens, they are often seen searching for earthworms with a waddling run along hedgerows and across lawns.

HABITAT Starlings are sociable and can often be seen flying in huge, swirling flocks, staying close together to ward off predators such as the Sparrowhawk. They will also join with migratory Starlings from Europe and form enormous flocks of thousands of birds, which can be seen swarming in the sky just before they settle to roost.

SWALLOW *Hirundo rustica*

ADULT Swallows of both sexes are similar in appearance, with a dark metallic blue on the wings, back, rump and tail. The tail is deeply forked and elongated, and is longest in older males. The Swallow has a deep red face, with blue covering the eyes, and a pale cream breast and underside. The wings are long and triangular, and the bills are short and pointed.

JUVENILE Juvenile Swallows resemble the adults, although the colours are less vibrant, the red face is paler and the tail shorter.

EGGS Swallows nest in overhangs on houses, bridges and other man-made structures. Both males and females build the nest, a hollow structure made from mud. Incubation lasts 14 to 16 days, with the female incubating alone. The eggs are glossy white with red speckles. Once these are hatched, both parents leave the nest to catch insects on the wing, which they collect in their throats until they return to their young. Once the young are fledged, they are fed in mid-air by the parents until they can hunt their own food.

SONG The Swallow's song is a warbling, twittering sound which can sometimes be mistaken for that of the Sparrow.

LENGTH	17–20 cm (6½–8 in)
WINGSPAN	30–35 cm (12–14 in)
BREEDING STARTS	**April**
NUMBER OF EGGS PER CLUTCH	**3–8**

J
F
M
A
M
J
J
A
S
O
N
D

Where in UK
Swallows
can be seen

Months when
Swallows
can be seen

DIET Swallows do not land to eat. They hunt and eat a variety of airborne insects – such as greenfly, bluebottles and horseflies – in mid-air. When feeding, they tend to fly low to the ground or skim over ponds and lakes to drink.

HABITAT Swallows are migratory birds and are only present during the summer. However they are then common and widespread.

OTHER Swallows are usually spotted wheeling and slipping from side to side in the air, where their long forked tails allow them amazing maneuverability. But when they land to collect mud for their nests, they can appear nervous and somewhat unsteady. Swallows often appear in huge flocks when they are preparing to fly south for the winter, gathering in their thousands to roost and circle in the sky before embarking on a journey which can take over two days with no opportunity for resting.

SWIFT *Apus apus*

ADULT Swifts are summer visitors which migrate from Africa. They have a short, forked tail and long, scythe-shaped wings. Their bodies are narrow and their heads small and blunt. They are dark brown all over, with a pale chin. Their beaks and legs are short, so short in fact, that they cannot take off from the ground. Their scientific name is derived from Ancient Greek, meaning 'without feet'.

JUVENILE Adults and juveniles are alike in appearance.

EGGS They nest under the eaves of houses using grass, leaves and feathers, which are bonded with saliva. They will sometimes use a nesting box if provided. Nesting is the only time that Swifts stop flying. Incubation lasts around 19 or 20 days, and both the male and female incubate the eggs, which are smooth and white. When the young hatch, both parents also share feeding duties.

SONG A Swift's call is a high-pitched screech. You can often hear this as numbers of them chase each other through the summer sky, with a twitchy flight pattern mixed with long glides.

DIET Swifts eat airborne insects and flies, as well as young spiderlings, which are carried on the wind. When they are feeding, they fly more slowly than when chasing each other.

LENGTH	15 cm (6 in)
WINGSPAN	25–28 cm (10–11 in)
BREEDING STARTS	April
NUMBER OF EGGS PER CLUTCH	3–8

Where in UK Swifts can be seen	Months when Swifts can be seen

HABITAT Swifts prefer towns to the countryside, although they are associated with both habitats. They are a common sight in summer, often seen as silhouettes high in the sky or swooping low over rooftops before settling to roost.

OTHER Swifts undertake long flights in and out of the country every year, and birds as young as 48 hours old have been found thousands of miles from where they hatched. They have incredible stamina, and can even sleep whilst flying. They fly extremely quickly, and have been recorded reaching speeds of up to 137 miles per hour. Swifts are also thought to be reliable indicators of thunderstorms; flying away from approaching bad weather.

WREN *Troglodytes troglodytes*

ADULT The Wren is an energetic little garden bird. A rusty brown colour with a long pale stripe above the eye, the Wren has light brown bars on its wings and a pale breast and underside. The tail is short and broad, and is often cocked and flicked repeatedly. The bill is brown, and is long and thin for probing cracks and crevices for food. Wrens have a round, dumpy frame.

JUVENILE Juvenile Wrens are similar to adults, although the stripe above the eye is not as prominent until they are mature.

EGGS Wrens nest in trees, holes, and even other birds' nests. They use leaves, grass and moss to build their round, globe-shaped nest, which the female lines with feathers. The eggs, when laid, are white and covered in red spots. The female incubates these alone for 13 to 18 days, although both parents play a part in feeding the young.

SONG The Wren has a very loud, distinctive song: a mix of trilling and warbling, finishing with a flourish. When singing, the Wren's body will tremble due to the amount of effort being exerted. They sing loudly in relation to their size, owing to a hollow cavity in their chest which allows sound to reverberate and amplify. Their alarm call is a loud tek-tek-tek.

LENGTH	9–10cm (3½–4 in)
WINGSPAN	13–17cm (5–6½ in)
BREEDING STARTS	April
NUMBER OF EGGS PER CLUTCH	5–8

J
F
M
A
M
J
J
A
S
O
N
D

Where in UK Wrens can be seen

Months when Wrens can be seen

DIET Wrens are insectivorous and mainly eat spiders, insects, and flies. They can be seen hopping along on the ground, using their long bill to probe cracks and holes searching for food. When feeding on open ground, they dart quickly from place to place. They can also be spotted taking bread and cheese from bird tables, although they rarely use hanging feeders.

HABITAT Wrens are very hardy and adaptable birds, and although commonest in gardens, they are widespread. They make use of human offerings, roosting in loft cavities in houses, and in nesting boxes, especially during colder weather.

OTHER Although Wrens are very small, they are lively and can often be seen creeping, jumping and dashing through undergrowth.

PROVIDING FOR BIRDS IN THE GARDEN

Birds will visit a garden where they feel safe, and where there is something to attract them, such as food, water and a safe place to nest. The more of this you can provide, the more likely birds are to visit. Safety is provided by cover in the form of shrubs, a hedge or trees – the more the better. Off the ground and away from ground-based predators, birds can perch, court, feed their young, or simply rest. Gardens with some sort of cover definitely attract more birds than those with little or no cover.

Shrubs, hedges and trees also provide an opportunity to hang nesting boxes or roosting pouches – although sometimes a fence or wall can be used. A good supplier will tell you what kind of box attracts what kind of bird, and how and where to hang it. The most important points are to prevent the eggs or nestlings from roasting in the midday sun by facing the box east or west, and to keep it safe from predators such as badgers or climbing cats.

Providing food

If you have a garden full of shrubs and flowering plants you will be providing food for birds indirectly – birds will eat the food they are adapted for, whether this is aphids, beetles, slugs and worms that live among your plants, or the seeds produced by them. But you can augment this provision by putting out food specially for the birds.

Bird tables offer a safe place to find food, although you may need to find a way to stop cats from climbing it. A table should have a raised edge to stop food falling off, and drainage for rainwater. Clean tables and regularly remove old food and droppings which can spread disease between birds.

Place table feeders in open ground with good all-round vision. This allows users to look out for birds of prey such as Sparrowhawks; and birds which prefer to forage on the ground below, such as Blackbirds, can avoid predation by cats.

If you use nut feeders, avoid ones with soft plastic netting as birds' feet can become caught. A firm metal mesh, or a solid cylinder with feeding holes is better. If you go for mesh, the holes should be small enough to stop whole nuts being removed as these can choke young birds.

Providing a variety of food gives you a better chance of attracting a more diverse range of birds. Hanging feeders filled with sunflower seeds and peanuts are popular with Nuthatches and larger finches such as the Hawfinch and Bullfinch. Smaller seeds such as niger, millet and linseed will be enjoyed by Sparrows, Tits and smaller finches.

On tables you can offer lard, fat and unsalted butter, or suet cake, to provide energy for birds which normally feed on insects, such as Tits, Robins and Woodpeckers. Blackbirds, Thrushes, Robins and Starlings will eat fruit such as apples, pears and bananas if placed on the ground. These birds will also enjoy feeding on mealworms if provided.

If you have larger birds such as Collared Doves or Wood Pigeons in your garden, you can feed them crushed oats, wheat and other grain.

When to feed

Feeding garden birds should ideally be a year-round activity. In winter birds can find it difficult to find their usual sources of food and appreciate a little extra help. Feeding birds in spring and summer provides extra nutrition, which helps birds moult and of course helps parents with their huge task of bringing up young.

In late summer and autumn you may find birds use your table and feeders less, as nature is then providing an abundance of berries, seeds and insects. But this is a key time for migratory birds, when they will look to feed as much as possible in preparation for the long journey to their wintering grounds. So keep on feeding for their benefit.

Valuable water

Food should always be accompanied by a source of water. The easiest way is to provide a bird bath, which birds will drink from and bathe in. Clean this out regularly, to keep it from spreading disease. If you can provide a pond, that will increase the appeal of your garden to birds hugely.

Ponds are a source of water for all wildlife, and will attract a variety of water life and insects. This in turn will attract birds such as Robins and Tits. Blackbirds and Thrushes will also take advantage of slugs and snails drawn to the water, and you may even have Swallows and House Martins visiting to steal insects from the water or to gather mud for their nests.

LESS COMMON BIRDS

Siskin *Carduelis spinus*

The Siskin is a garden visitor. The adult male is a yellow-green colour with a black cap and bib. The breast is yellow, fading to white on the underside, and the wings are mainly black, with a broad yellow band which is distinctive in flight. Adult females are yellow-brown, with a white breast that is streaked with brown and lacking the black cap and bib. Juveniles are browner than the adult female, and the brown streaks are more prominent.

Siskins nest in conifers and generally eat cone seeds, such as spruce, birch and pine. As such, they find plenty of food in woodland. However, they will visit gardens during winter to find nuts and seeds. Like the Blue Tit, they will hang acrobatically from these feeders as they eat.

Breeding was until recently restricted to pine forests in north-east Scotland. However, the birds have spread southward and are now nesting in many English counties as well.

Jackdaw *Corvus monedula*

Adult Jackdaws of both sexes are a pale grey on the cheeks and nape, with a very dark grey on the wings and tail. The bill is black, as is a distinctive cap which also covers the eye. Juveniles are similar, although a darker grey.

Jackdaws are widespread across the country and are a common sight in fields and around the edge of woodland. Like most crows, the Jackdaw is omnivorous and can find food in any environment although it suffers from competition with larger crows. They will visit larger gardens in order to raid the eggs from pigeons' nests, and will sometimes take food put out for smaller garden birds; they can often be seen flying over gardens when travelling to feeding grounds.

Goldfinch *Carduelis carduelis*

The Goldfinch is a mixture of yellow, white, brown and red. The face has red around the bill, with some white and black. The nape and back are brown, and the wings dark brown, with yellow bands across. The adult male has bright white on the face, whereas the female is a very dull cream. Juveniles are similar to adult females, but lack the red face markings.

Goldfinches are not averse to visiting gardens, especially wilder ones – their preferred food is weed seeds such as dandelion and thistle. They may take sunflower hearts from feeders, or their favourite niger seeds.

Goldfinch numbers took a sharp decline in the 1970s and 1980s due to the increased use of herbicides to eradicate weeds, and agricultural practices still continue to threaten this charming bird.

Dunnock *Prunella modularis*

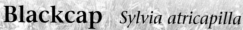

The Dunnock (also known as the Hedge Sparrow) resembles the Tree Sparrow with its dark brown colouring. The adult male Dunnock has a blue-grey colouring around its face and on the breast. Its brown back and wings are streaked with a darker brown. The adult female is similar, but has a shorter tail. Juveniles are mottled brown with a buff breast and dark brown streaks. The bill is dark in adults, and light in juveniles.

Dunnocks often appear nervous and agitated, with wings and tails flicking as they search for food on the ground. They are primarily a woodland bird and remain close to cover in gardens when looking for beetles, ants, spiders, seeds or berries. This diet is similar to the Robin's and as a result Robins, which are fiercely territorial, will chase Dunnocks away from 'their' garden territory.

Blackcap *Sylvia atricapilla*

Blackcaps are migratory birds which winter in Africa. The males have grey upper parts and are pale below, with a blue face and, as the name suggests, a black cap. Females have a more reddish-brown cap and they are browner overall. Juveniles are similar to females except their cap is darker.

Blackcaps usually live in woodland, where they feed mainly on insects, spiders and caterpillars, seeds and berries. They occasionally visit bird tables in the winter, and may feed from suet bars, especially those packed with dried flies.

WOODLAND AND FARMLAND BIRDS

Thousands of years ago the UK was virtually covered in woodland, and was surely full of woodland birds as a result. Over many centuries woods have been cut down and dug up to make way for farmland and for towns, and today's woods are much smaller than they once were. Yet woodlands are still an important place for birds as well as for humans, and the possibility of spotting a Coal Tit or Jay, or of hearing a Cuckoo, makes a ramble in the woods all the more enjoyable.

THE WOODLAND AND FARMLAND HABITAT

Up until about 5,000 years ago, the UK was almost completely covered in forest, mostly oak and elm. Then the Neolithic people began to clear the trees to enable agriculture and settlement. Since then, more and more of our woodland has disappeared and with it have gone many bird species. Today, even though some forest has been replanted, most of the countryside is human-made, and just about every species of bird that has survived the removal of the original forests has had to adapt in some way to this new environment.

Studies show that for some species of woodland, birds numbers have gone down by as much as 20% in the past 20 years alone. These include the Nightingale, the Lesser Spotted Woodpecker and the Wryneck. In fact, the RSPB believes that the Lesser Spotted Woodpecker and the Wryneck are no longer breeding in the UK. However, some bird species have increased their numbers, including Blackcaps, Magpies and Collared Doves.

Adapting to habitat

One of the most obvious ways in which birds such as the Chiffchaff have adapted to what woodland has, and has not, got to offer is by migrating. In the winter when insect reserves are low, these birds simply move to warmer climates for better food sources. Resident birds such as the Bullfinch manage by eating insects in the summer months and nuts and seeds in the winter.

Certain species of Owl have adapted to loss of dense forest by moving into smaller areas of woodland close to farmland. Here, in the less dense woodland, they are able to seek out prey such as field mice more easily.

As woodland has thinned and merged with urban developments, it is those birds able to thrive in both environments that have fared best. Traditional countryside birds such as Finches and Tits have long been seen congregating around the suburban bird table. Now the Wood Pigeon and Collared Dove are adapting to suburban and urban life and have increased their numbers hugely – even Green Woodpeckers can sometimes be seen on garden lawns. Much of this adaptation consists of learning to 'commute' from woodland to city for feeding purposes.

Nearly all woodland birds have undergone a noticeable change in wing shape. As woodland has become more fragmented, birds living in this habitat have developed more pointed wings. The generally accepted explanation is that pointed wings are associated with sustained flight, so as woodland becomes more fragmented, birds with more pointed wings are better able to travel the longer distances from one segment of woodland to another.

What the future holds

Even though major conservation efforts are being made, woodland is still being broken up and lost. In Wales, for example, there is a growing trend towards woodland being sold off in lots, and this fragmentation can affect the most vulnerable species that are least suited to interaction with humans.

The Lesser Spotted Woodpecker, Cuckoo, Hawfinch and Nightingale have not been able to adapt and their numbers are now becoming dangerously low, although the precise reasons for this are not fully understood. Further declines are being seen in woodland bird species in west Africa, where their habitat is being destroyed as more intensive farming techniques take hold, and climate change makes the journey across hot desert regions more difficult than before.

Different species of bird inhabit different types of woodland; restoration and replanting of new woodland will not help birds that depend on ancient woodland. This type of woodland cannot be replaced in the short term, so the only way to protect this environment is through strict conservation of remaining fragments. The reconnection of a patchwork of woodland is also an important step in reviving flagging species of birds normally found in large woodland areas. Unless this is done the sounds of many birds, such as the once-familiar call of the Cuckoo, may disappear forever from our countryside.

BRAMBLING *Fringella montifringella*

ADULT The Brambling is a finch, very similar to the Chaffinch, which changes colour through the seasons. In summer, the adult male has a black head, bill, wings and back, an orange breast and a streak of white on the rump. Its orange breast colouring also partially extends onto the wing. In summer, the black colouring changes to brown and the bill changes from black to yellow. The summer female is similar to the male but duller, but in winter its bill becomes brighter yellow and its head and cheeks develop a grey surrounding. This sometime leads to confusion with the Chaffinch.

JUVENILE Juvenile Bramblings appear similar to the adult female in winter, though they are lighter in colour.

EGGS Nests are built by the female, usually in a conifer tree close to the trunk. The nest is cup-shaped, constructed from moss, grass and hair, and lined with feathers and wool. The female will also decorate the nest using bark and lichen, which also serves to make the nest less conspicuous. Eggs vary between shades of green and brown, with dark brown markings, and the female will incubate them alone for 11 or 12 days. After hatching, the young are fed by both parents.

SONG The Brambling's call is a loud, buzzing *dzzairr* and a hard *tep* in flight.

LENGTH	**14 cm (5½ in)**
WINGSPAN	**24–26 cm (9½–10 in)**
BREEDING STARTS	**May**
NUMBER OF EGGS PER CLUTCH	**5–7**

J
F
M
A
M
J
J
A
S
O
N
D

Where in UK Brambling can be seen

Months when Brambling can be seen

DIET Bramblings eat beech mast, seeds and berries through the autumn and winter, and insects in summer. They will usually feed in trees when breeding, only occasionally venturing to the ground. They can be seen in enormous flocks in winter, when many Bramblings gather together in search of the best feeding grounds.

HABITAT Bramblings are migratory, only visiting the UK from Siberia and Scandinavia during the winter. They may sometimes be spotted in gardens in winter, if food in their preferred coniferous woodland is scarce, and they often join flocks with Chaffinches to search for food sources.

OTHER It has been known for some Bramblings to migrate to southern Europe in search of beech mast, one of their preferred food sources.

BULLFINCH *Pyrrhula pyrrhula*

ADULT The Bullfinch is a stocky, heavy finch which lives amongst dense undergrowth. It is a very colourful bird. Adults have a black cap which extends past the eye to the base of the blunt bill, which is also black. The wings are a pale blue-grey with a bar of similar colour, and a white rump lies at the top of a slightly forked black tail. The distinctive rose-pink breast is brighter in males than females. In both, the breast fades to white on the underside.

JUVENILE Juvenile Bullfinches resemble the adult female, however they lack the black cap and have a pale brown breast rather than pink.

EGGS The female Bullfinch builds a nest in a dense bush such as hawthorn or blackthorn, using twigs and moss. It lines the nest with hair and fine roots, then lays light blue eggs which it incubates for around 12 to 14 days. When these hatch, the male assists the female with feeding duties.

SONG The Bullfinch's song is high, trilling and sometimes mournful. The call is a short, piping *phew*.

LENGTH	14–16 cm (5½–6 in)
WINGSPAN	22–29 cm (9–12 in)
BREEDING STARTS	April
NUMBER OF EGGS PER CLUTCH	4–7

Where in UK Bullfinches can be seen

Months when Bullfinches can be seen

Female

Male

DIET Bullfinches have a short, powerful beak which is well adapted for eating seeds. They will also eat insects, berries, fruit and buds, which has seen the Bullfinch become unpopular with agriculturalists and gardeners. If they visit a garden, they will sometimes take seed from hanging feeders.

HABITAT It is often easier to hear a Bullfinch than see one, as they are retiring birds and do not venture far from dense cover. However, they can sometimes be spotted around the edge of woodland.

OTHER The Bullfinch was once on the decline as deer populations increased and fed on the greenery that provided these birds with low-lying cover. Bullfinches were also viewed as a pest and caught. Nowadays, this practice is fortunately rare and their numbers are quickly increasing again.

CHIFFCHAFF *Phylloscopus collybita*

ADULT In spring and summer, the male Chiffchaff is olive-green above, and creamy white below. It has a pale stripe (a supercilium) above the eye, and also an eye ring of similar colour. Adult females are similar to the male. In all Chiffchaffs, the legs and bills are dark. They are very like Willow Warblers. However there are some features which can be used to tell them apart: the supercilium is brighter in Willow Warblers, the tail of the Chiffchaff tends to wag rather than flick, and the Chiffchaff's wings are shorter.

JUVENILE Juveniles of both sexes are similar in appearance to the adults, though they have a more yellowish colouring on the underside.

EGGS The female builds a nest on the ground, usually in long grass or bushes, using plant matter and lining it with feathers. Eggs are smooth and white with purple or black markings. Incubation lasts 13 or 14 days and is performed by the female alone.

SONG The Chiffchaff's song is a shrill *chiff chaff chiff chaff*, from which it takes its common name. The call is a repeated, high-pitched *hweet*.

DIET Chiffchaffs primarily eat insects such as midges, caterpillars and moths. They can often be seen hunting for prey in tree canopies and amongst bushes. Its scientific name means 'leaf explorer', and this is reflected in the searching of the underside of leaves for aphids.

LENGTH	10–11 cm (4 in)
WINGSPAN	15–21 cm (6–8 in)
BREEDING STARTS	April
NUMBER OF EGGS PER CLUTCH	4–9

North	South
J	J
F	F
M	M
A	A
M	M
J	J
J	J
A	A
S	S
O	O
N	N
D	D

Where in UK Chiffchaffs can be seen

Months when Chiffchaffs can be seen

HABITAT The Chiffchaff is a warbler, which is resident in the southern areas of Britain and visits more northerly areas following migration from the Mediterranean and Africa in summer.

OTHER Chiffchaffs are very active and can often be seen speeding through trees in search of food. They can appear slightly nervous and restless – another good way to tell them apart from the Willow Warbler.

COAL TIT *Periparus ater*

ADULT The Coal Tit is similar to the Blue Tit but much less colourful. The adults of both sexes have a black cap and bill, with a white nape, breast and cheeks. The back is a light grey, as are the wings, which have two white bars across them. The white breast leads to a yellowish underside, with blue-grey legs.

JUVENILE Juvenile Coal Tits are similar to their parents, but appear slightly browner above.

EGGS Like other Tits, the Coal Tit mostly nests in tree hollows, though it has been known to nest in mouse holes, old Magpie nests and even squirrel dreys. The nest is made from moss and other plant matter, lined with feathers and sometimes rabbit fur. Eggs are white and smooth with reddish-brown speckles. The female incubates alone for around 14 to 16 days, after which the young are fed by both parents.

SONG When feeding, Coal Tits will keep in almost constant contact with others with a short *see-see*. The song is a high-pitched *pee-chew*, which is similar to that of the Great Tit, but quicker.

DIET Coal Tits mainly eat seeds common to conifer forests, such as beech mast, and those found in fir and larch cones. They also eat insects, and will occasionally visit gardens where they will eat sunflower seeds if available.

LENGTH	11.5 cm (4½ in)
WINGSPAN	17 cm–21 cm (6½–8½ in)
BREEDING STARTS	April
NUMBER OF EGGS PER CLUTCH	1–2

Where in UK Coal Tits can be seen	Months when Coal Tits can be seen

HABITAT You are likely to see a Coal Tit in woodland hopping around in high trees searching for food. If they visit a garden, they often use hanging feeders to feed acrobatically, like other small tits.

OTHER Coal Tits have a peculiar habit of hoarding food when it is plentiful in order to draw on these reserves during hard times through the winter. Unfortunately, they often forget where they have hidden their supplies. Great Tits have also been seen watching where Coal Tits hide their food, and then moving in to steal it later.

SPOTTED FLYCATCHER *Muscicapa striata*

ADULT The Spotted Flycatcher is a common woodland bird, and all ages and sexes have a very similar appearance. They are slim birds, with grey-brown colouring above. The throat, breast and underside are cream with brown speckling. The bill and legs are black.

JUVENILE Juveniles are very like the adults but have speckling on the head and spots on the back, both cream in colour.

EGGS Both parents build a cup-shaped nest from grass, twigs and lichen, lining it with feathers and hair. The usual site is the angle between a tree branch and trunk in woodland, but nests have been found in gardens and parks with a large number of trees. Flycatchers will also sometimes use open-fronted nesting boxes if available. Eggs are white with red blotches and the female will incubate them alone for 11 to 15 days.

SONG The Spotted Flycatcher's call is a high-pitched but quiet *tsee, tsee*, which is used frequently.

LENGTH	**15 cm (6 in)**
WINGSPAN	**23–25 cm (9–10 in)**
BREEDING STARTS	**May**
NUMBER OF EGGS PER CLUTCH	**1–2**

J
F
M
A
M
J
J
A
S
O
N
D

Where in UK Spotted Flycatchers can be seen

Months when Spotted Flycatcher can be seen

DIET As the name suggests, the Spotted Flycatcher mainly eats flying insects such as flies, bees and butterflies. They will also eat berries when available towards the end of summer, before leaving for warmer climes.

HABITAT It is easy to see a Spotted Flycatcher during the summer, when they are present across most of the country; in autumn they migrate, wintering in Africa and south western Asia. They can often be found around the edge of woodland or in trees in gardens and parks.

OTHER Flycatchers will choose an exposed branch to perch on, and wait there for flying insects to pass by. Then they dart out to catch their prey before returning to the perch to wait again. They tend to perch very straight and upright when hunting like this, flicking their tails impatiently.

GREEN WOODPECKER *Picus viridis*

ADULT   The Green Woodpecker is a large, bold bird with vibrant plumage, a boisterous voice and ebullient character. In both male and female, the bright green colour is accentuated by a yellow rump, a vivid red crown, and a black cheek and facial mask surrounding the eye. The female's mask is all black, whereas the male's has a red centre. Large grey feet with long claws, a strong spiny tail and a long black beak give it the essential tools for the trade as a Woodpecker.

JUVENILE   Juvenile Green Woodpeckers can be much more spotted overall, with a grey face and less distinct facial markings.

EGGS   As with the rest of the woodpecker family, Green Woodpeckers nest in holes in mature trees. The eggs are smooth, glossy and white. Both adults incubate the eggs for about 18 days, and share the feeding once the young have hatched.

LENGTH	**30–33 cm (12–13 in)**
WINGSPAN	**40–42 cm (16–17 in)**
BREEDING STARTS	**late April**
NUMBER OF EGGS PER CLUTCH	**4–9**

J F M A M J J A S O N D

Where in UK
Green Woodpeckers
can be seen

Months when
Green Woodpecke
can be seen

SONG   Should the bird be disturbed, it flies off alternately flapping and folding its wings on a low undulating flight; the bird heads for the cover of trees whilst shrieking its signature yaffle in alarm. This call is a shrill but unique series of 10–20 laughing *kyu* calls, increasing in speed and slightly in pitch towards the end.

DIET   Whilst it resembles the other woodpeckers, the Green Woodpecker is somewhat misnamed as it spends most of the time drilling for ants and insects in open grasslands. It commonly hops along the ground, propping itself up on its spiny tail as it stretches tall to keep watch all around, then probing the ground with its sharp black bill. Upon finding ants or grubs under the surface it will drill for more, pushing down left and right with all its strength, digging into the ground to the full depth of its bill, sometimes getting quite dirty in the process.

HABITAT   Green Woodpeckers inhabit open or mixed woodlands, farmland and moors, and are commonly found in parks and gardens.

OTHER   Usually solitary, the Green Woodpecker occasionally drums on a hollow tree to advertize its presence to others in the area. The drumming is fast, but surprisingly gentle and short in duration by comparison with the Greater Spotted Woodpecker.

HAWFINCH *Coccothraustes coccothraustes*

ADULT The Hawfinch is a heavily built member of the finch family, with a large head, strong, conical bill and a short, powerful neck. Adult males and females look alike, with black around the eyes and a rusty-brown back. The head is orange-brown, as are the breast and underside, and it has a blue-grey nape. The wings are dark with a broad white diagonal stripe, and white bars across the secondary feathers, which are visible in flight. The Hawfinch has black around the eyes, a short tail, a blue-grey bill and pink legs.

JUVENILE Juveniles have a more orange colouring on the head and lack black markings. Also, the breast is more grey-yellow, and dark spots are present on the underside.

EGGS Nests are constructed in tree forks, usually in an area of deciduous woodland or orchards, and are a shallow, saucer shape. The female incubates the eggs alone for 9 to 14 days. These eggs are light blue or grey-green in colour with black markings. Once hatched, the young are fed by both parents.

SONG Their call is a quiet *tic, tic.*

DIET Hawfinches mainly eat seeds, such as hornbeam and beech. They also eat hips and haws of hedgerows. In spring they eat oak buds, and then in summer they eat insects such as beetles. They can use their powerful bill to crush cherry stones to eat the seed within, which is a favoured food of the Hawfinch.

LENGTH	18 cm (7 in)
WINGSPAN	29–33 cm (11½ –13 in)
BREEDING STARTS	April
NUMBER OF EGGS PER CLUTCH	2–7

J
F
M
A
M
J
J
A
S
O
N
D

Where in UK
Hawfinches
can be seen

Months when
Hawfinches
can be seen

HABITAT Hawfinches are reclusive birds and can be difficult to spot. They can mainly be seen high in tree canopies, flying the short distance to other tree tops, rather than moving across longer distances closer to the ground.

OTHER Hawfinches can exert a huge amount of pressure using their strong bills and necks, which allows them to feed on a range of seeds which other birds cannot reach. When crushing cherry stones, they can apply a force equivalent to a human exerting pressure of up to 60 tonnes.

JAY   *Garrulus glandarius*

ADULT   The Jay is a member of the crow family. Unlike other crows, the Jay is brightly coloured. Predominantly a pinkish-brown, the head has a black and white flecked crown with a white throat and a black 'moustache' at the base of the bill, which is long, thick and dark. The wings are black, with striking blue patches and a band of white across them, which is very distinctive in flight. The rump is white, and the tail is quite long and black.

JUVENILE   Jays of all ages and sexes look the same, with little way to distinguish male from female, or adult from juvenile.

EGGS   Both male and female build the nest, usually in a tree or shrub. This nest appears quite untidy, and is made from twigs and lined with roots and hair. The female then lays blue-green or olive green eggs, which have buff speckling. Incubation is performed by the female for up to 16 or 17 days. After hatching, both parents feed the young.

SONG   Jays have an almost chattering song, which is a mixture of squeaks and chirrups. Their alarm call is a harsh *krar, krar* sound. Jays are quite shy and wary, and can often be heard without being seen. It is common to hear a Jay's alarm call as it flashes through the trees.

LENGTH	35 cm (14 in)
WINGSPAN	52–58 cm (20½–23 in)
BREEDING STARTS	April
NUMBER OF EGGS PER CLUTCH	3–10

Where in UK Jays can be seen

Months when Jays can be seen

DIET   Like other crows, Jays are omnivorous and will eat a wide variety of foods including fruit, berries, eggs and nuts. They eat acorns, which they hoard in crevices or beneath the ground. And they will hunt insects, small rodents, newts and even bats and young birds.

HABITAT   Jays never stray far from tree cover in their woodland haunts, unless they must search further afield for food.

OTHER   Jays are very social birds and in spring can form groups of up to 30 birds. These are unmated birds seeking partners. Smaller groups may be an unmated female courted by unmated males. Once a mate is found, the pair will stay together for life. Jays are known to be quite intelligent and, like other crows, have the capacity for problem-solving. They are better than many species at finding again the food which they have buried for times of hardship.

LONG-TAILED TIT *Aegithalos caudatus*

ADULT The Long-tailed Tit is a tiny bird with a long, thin tail and a short, round body. The adults of both sexes are similar: dark brown above, with a dark tail. They have a pinkish breast and underside. The head is white, with a black crown. This white colouring becomes flecked with black around the eye, which has a red ring around it. The bill is small and black, and legs are black-brown. Interestingly, the Long-tailed Tit's appearance varies between locations. In northern Europe, the white head lacks the black band, and they appear more grey on the breast and underside.

JUVENILE Juvenile Long-tailed Tits are similar in appearance to adults, but lack the colouring in the breast, which remains white. They also have a brown crown on the head, rather than a black one, and their face is more grey than white.

EGGS The Long-tailed Tit's nest is a ball-shaped construction of lichen, feathers, spider web and hair, usually constructed in a bush, hedge or tree. Brambles and gorse bushes are particular favourites as nesting sites. The nest is built by both male and female, and can take up to three weeks to complete. The female then incubates the eggs, which are white with purplish-red spots, for 12 to 14 days. Both adults help feed the young.

LENGTH	15 cm (6 in)
WINGSPAN	17–19 cm (7–7½ in)
BREEDING STARTS	April
NUMBER OF EGGS PER CLUTCH	5–16

Where in UK
Long-tailed Tits
can be seen

Months when
Long-tailed Tits
can be seen

SONG The song of the Long-tailed Tit is a chirruping, trilling sound, but it is most easily identifiable by its high-pitched *tsee-tsee-tsee-tsee* contact call.

DIET Long-tailed Tits eat insects and larvae, spiders and berries.

HABITAT In gardens, you may be lucky enough to see Long-tailed Tits eating nuts from hanging feeders. The most likely place to see a Long-tailed Tit, however, is in woodland and farmland hedgerows.

OTHER Long-tailed Tits are very social, like other tits, and often gather in small flocks of up to 20 birds. In winter they will join much larger flocks with other tit species in search of food. The tail of the Long-tailed Tit accounts for over half of its length, which means that the Long-tailed tit has the longest tail of any of our birds in proportion to its body.

MISTLE THRUSH   *Turdus viscivorus*

ADULT   The Mistle Thrush is a larger, more aggressive relative of the Song Thrush. It is paler than the Song Thrush, but has similar spotted markings on the breast. The adult Mistle Thrush of both sexes is grey-brown above, with a pale buff breast and underside which is covered in large, dark brown spots. The wings are grey-brown above and pale on the underside. There are also pale tips to the wing feathers, which give the impression of the wings having a pale patch from a distance.

JUVENILE   Juveniles are similar to the adults, but have a paler head and smaller spots on the breast.

EGGS   Mistle Thrushes usually nest in the fork of a tree, but will sometimes use shrubs or gaps in walls. The female builds the nest from grass, roots, moss and earth, and incubates the eggs for 12 to 15 days. Both parents help to feed the young.

SONG   The song of the Mistle Thrush is pleasant and fluty, and quite loud. It can be far-reaching, and is often heard during bad weather – leading to another of its names, the Stormcock. The call is often heard in flight, a hard rattling noise similar to an old football rattle.

LENGTH	27 cm (11 in)
WINGSPAN	42–48 cm (16½–19 in)
BREEDING STARTS	February
NUMBER OF EGGS PER CLUTCH	3–6

Where in UK Mistle Thrushes can be seen

Months when Mistle Thrushes can be seen

DIET   Mistle Thrushes eat a wide variety of food: insects, worms, slugs and berries. Its diet is very similar to the Song Thrush's, except they eat fewer snails. In winter, they can be heard singing in order to defend a fruit-bearing tree – a valuable source of food through the winter.

HABITAT   Mistle Thrushes are common throughout woodland, hedgerows and farmland, in areas where there is plenty of cover. They travel short distances in search of food just above tree top height, flying with quick wing beats followed by a short glide.

OTHER   The population of Mistle Thrushes has diminished in the last 30 years, especially in farmland areas. The Mistle Thrush's Latin name means 'mistletoe eater'.

NUTHATCH   *Sitta europae*

ADULT   Nuthatches are small, compact birds. The adult male is a dark blue-grey across the head, nape, back and wings. The tail is also dark, with white corners. Below, the Nuthatch is a light red-orange on the breast and underside. The face is white, with a broad black stripe extending from the bill across the eye, and across the side of its large head. The bill is stout and pointed, and the tail is short and broad. Females are similar in appearance, but are slightly paler.

JUVENILE   Both sexes of juvenile Nuthatches are similar in appearance to the adults, but often have duller colourings.

EGGS   Nuthatches like to nest in a hole, usually in a tree or sometimes in a wall. Nests are built from bark and dead leaves, and the nesting hole may be reduced in size by adding layers of mud. They will also use the abandoned nests of other birds, or a nesting box if available. The eggs are white with red or brown spots. The female will incubate alone, for about 14 to 18 days, but both parents help to feed the hatchlings.

SONG   The song of the Nuthatch is a long series of rapid, piping notes of the same note. Its call is a steady *chit, chit, chit-chit*.

DIET   Nuthatches can be seen climbing on broad tree trunks looking for food. In summer, this is mainly spiders, insects and beetles, with berries and acorns being eaten in winter.

LENGTH	**15 cm (6 in)**
WINGSPAN	**20–25 cm (8–10 in)**
BREEDING STARTS	**April**
NUMBER OF EGGS PER CLUTCH	**1–2**

J
F
M
A
M
J
J
A
S
O
N
D

Where in UK Nuthatches can be seen

Months when Nuthatches can be seen

HABITAT   Nuthatches prefer woodland in England and Wales, although they are beginning to be seen in Scotland too. They occasionally visit gardens in search of food and may use hanging bird feeders.

OTHER   The Nuthatch's remarkable climbing ability is due to its strong legs. It is the only bird which can climb headfirst both up and down a tree trunk. It is able to move around trees and between trees very quickly, in search of food.

STOCK DOVE   *Columba oenas*

ADULT   The Stock Dove is very similar in appearance to both the common (feral) Pigeon and the larger Wood Pigeon. The Stock Dove of either sex is blue-grey across its head, back, wings and underside, with a dark tail. Its most distinctive feature is an iridescent bottle-green patch on its neck, and a pinkish patch above its pale grey breast. Its lack of a white patch on the neck helps distinguish it from the Wood Pigeon, as do the two black bars across its wings. In flight, the Stock Dove is pale beneath the wings, with a black band on the tips of the wings and tail. The eyes are black, and the bill is slightly curved and pointed.

JUVENILE   Juveniles are similar to adults but appear duller and lack the iridescent green patch.

EGGS   Stock Doves nest in holes in trees or buildings, in ivy, and even in rabbit burrows, as well as occasionally in nesting boxes. Nests are built from twigs and dead leaves and the eggs, when laid, are a cream colour. Both parents incubate the eggs for 16 to 18 days, and both feed the hatched young.

SONG   The Stock Dove's song is a low *ooo-uu-ooh*. The notes are short and deep.

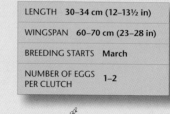

LENGTH	30–34 cm (12–13½ in)
WINGSPAN	60–70 cm (23–28 in)
BREEDING STARTS	March
NUMBER OF EGGS PER CLUTCH	1–2

Where in UK
Stock Doves
can be seen

Months when
Stock Doves
can be seen

DIET   The diet of the Stock Dove is almost completely vegetarian: leaves, tree and plant buds, berries, grain and seeds. Stock Doves will visit bird tables in search of seed and will occasionally eat insects and snails.

HABITAT   The best place to spot a Stock Dove is in woodland where there is plenty of ground cover. During winter, they can also be seen in large flocks with other types of pigeons and doves on farmland, where they will feed on grain.

OTHER   The Stock Dove is now common throughout Britain, although numbers declined steeply in the 1950s, possibly as a result of chemicals used to dress seeds for agricultural use. This decline was reversed by the late 1960s.

TREECREEPER *Certhia familiaris*

ADULT The Treecreeper is a small woodland bird with a mottled brown and golden yellow across its head, nape and wings. The rump is a rusty-brown colour, the tail is slightly darker than this and the face, breast and underside are creamy white. There is a pale brown stripe over the eye. The bill is thin and curved. Male and female Treecreepers are very similar in appearance.

JUVENILE It is difficult to distinguish between juvenile and mature Treecreepers as the colourings and markings are consistent across both age and sex.

EGGS Treecreepers build nests from twigs, grass and moss, usually behind loose tree bark or in creeping plants such as ivy. The female lays white eggs speckled with red and brown. She will incubate the eggs alone for 14 or 15 days. Both parents take on feeding responsibilities when the young hatch.

SONG The song is a sweet, lilting sound, with small, high-pitched notes usually finished with a flourish. When they fly between trees, they emit a shrill call, a piercing *tseee, tseee, tseee*, moving in a noticeably erratic pattern.

DIET Treecreepers are insectivorous and use their curved bill to probe the small cracks and crevices on tree trunks and branches in search of insects. They also eat some types of seed, such as pine and spruce.

LENGTH	**12.5 cm (5 in)**
WINGSPAN	**17–21 cm (7–8½ in)**
BREEDING STARTS	**April**
NUMBER OF EGGS PER CLUTCH	**3–9**

J
F
M
A
M
J
J
A
S
O
N
D

Where in UK Treecreepers can be seen

Months when Treecreepers can be seen

HABITAT Treecreepers spend a lot of their time searching for food in woodland; they rarely visit gardens. If you are looking for one, listen out for its call as it feeds in winter.

OTHER Treecreepers are generally quite solitary, but will often join others to roost in very cold weather. As the name suggests, they are experts at climbing trees, using their short tail for balance as they scurry up the trunk, usually in a spiral pattern. They are perfectly camouflaged from behind, so it may be the white breast which is spotted first.

WOOD PIGEON *Columba palumbus*

ADULT The Wood Pigeon is a large, long-tailed pigeon with a broad body and large head – in fact it is the largest pigeon in Europe. The adults of both sexes display the same colouring: mostly blue-grey on the upper parts, with a pinkish breast, and a bottle-green patch on the nape with a white patch alongside. In flight, the wings have a distinctive white band along their length, with black tips. The tail is also tipped with black.

JUVENILE Juvenile Wood Pigeons are like the adults, although their colouring is lighter. They also lack the white patch on the neck, which does not form until they are at least six months old. Juveniles are sometimes mistaken for the smaller Stock Dove. The bright red and yellow bill and yellow eyes of the Wood Pigeon help to tell them apart.

EGGS As other pigeons do, the Wood Pigeon builds a nest from twigs on a shallow, saucer-shaped platform in a high tree. This nest can appear very weak and unable to support the birds. Both parents share incubation of the white eggs and help to feed the young. In a breeding season, up to three clutches may be laid.

SONG Wood Pigeons have a distinctive call: *ru-hoo, ru, ru-hoo*. It can be distinguished from other doves and pigeons as it consists of five notes, whereas most other calls contain only three.

LENGTH	**40–42 cm (16–16½ in)**
WINGSPAN	**75–80 cm (29½–31½ in)**
BREEDING STARTS	**April**
NUMBER OF EGGS PER CLUTCH	**2**

J
F
M
A
M
J
J
A
S
O
N
D

Where in UK
Wood Pigeons
can be seen

Months when
Wood Pigeon
can be seen

DIET Wood Pigeons eat grain and weed seeds.

HABITAT The Wood Pigeon can be seen in woodland. It can also be found in groups on farmland, feeding on crop residues and seed; the bird's presence here has led to its reputation as a pest. Pigeons will also visit gardens, feeding on weed seeds and sometimes from bird tables.

OTHER Wood Pigeons spend a lot of time drinking, as their diets provide little moisture. They are different from many birds in that they use their beaks as a straw to drink: rather than tilt their head back, they drink with their head lowered. Another interesting feature of Wood Pigeons is that their feathers actually weigh more than their skeleton – a rare occurrence in birds.

WOOD WARBLER   *Phylloscopus sibilatrix*

ADULT The Wood Warbler is a small, brightly coloured bird. The adult male has a bright yellow face and breast, white underside and a darker supercilium across the eye; it is mainly green-yellow across the upperparts with dark tips to the wings and tail. The adult female is similar, although with a shorter body and tail. The pointed bill is orange-yellow, and the legs are dark brown.

JUVENILE Juvenile Wood Warblers are similar to adults, but have white tips to the primary wing feathers and a darker bill.

EGGS Wood Warblers build nests from roots, moss and other plant matter, near the ground, usually in low shrubs or in holes on the ground. Eggs are white with reddish-brown or black markings. Incubation lasts around 13 days, and is carried out by the female alone. However, both parents feed the young, usually with each parent feeding half of the chicks.

SONG The song of the Wood Warbler has sharp, ticking notes which eventually merge into a fast trill: *t-t-ti-tit-titititirrrrrr*. This is sometimes interspersed with a *pew, pew, pew*, which can sound almost melancholy. The call is a repeated *swee, swee, swee*.

LENGTH	22 cm (8½ in)
WINGSPAN	37–42 cm (14½–17 in)
BREEDING STARTS	May
NUMBER OF EGGS PER CLUTCH	5–6

Where in UK
Wood Warblers
can be seen

Months when
Wood Warblers
can be seen

DIET Wood Warblers mainly eat insects, but will also feed on berries, seeds and fruit. Their pointed bill allows them to access insects in cracks and gaps in trees.

HABITAT Common in deciduous woodland, Wood Warblers can be seen searching for food at all heights – whether on the ground, in bushes and shrubs, or in tree canopies. They prefer areas which are covered by canopy but are open beneath, which allows them to fly easily between trees. They are migratory visitors, so the best time of year to see them is during the warm summer months.

OTHER As they are very active, Wood Warblers spend a lot of time feeding to maintain their energy levels. Though brightly coloured, Wood Warblers are quite reclusive. It can sometimes be tricky to spot them, but you may hear the high-pitched song before you see them.

LESS COMMON BIRDS

CUCKOO   *Cuculus canorus*

The Cuckoo is a summer visitor. Adult male Cuckoos are mainly blue-grey, with horizontal barring on the underside. The tail is tipped with black. The female is very different; the back and wings are red-brown above with dark brown bars across. There is a small white band on the nape, and the face and breast are a pale cream, again with brown barred plumage. Juveniles look like the female, but are a very dark brown.

The Cuckoo has suffered a dip in numbers. This may seem surprising, as its habit of replacing other birds' eggs with its own would suggest it had a good survival strategy – remarkably, each individual female lays eggs which are similar to a particular species of bird, rather than simply laying an egg in a random nest. It has been suggested that the fall in numbers of other birds may be responsible for the fall in Cuckoo numbers, as there are fewer and fewer hosts for Cuckoo eggs.

The cuckoo call is made by the male as it perches, and is the best indicator of its presence. They are distinctive when at rest, with the tail pointed up and the wings drooping.

NIGHTINGALE   *Luscinia megarhynchos*

Another summer visitor is the Nightingale. A reclusive bird, which spends a lot of time in woodland thickets, the adult Nightingale is a plain brown colour above, and a paler brown below. The primary wing feathers are tipped in black, and there is a pale ring around the eye. Juveniles appear more mottled above, and have an orange-brown breast. The same colour is also present beneath the tail on Nightingales of all ages. Like the Cuckoo, its wings often droop down beside its broad body.

Nightingales eat insects, which are abundant during the summer, and so they rarely move far from their territory. It is uncommon to see a Nightingale flying between feeding grounds. The famous song is an unmistakable series of rapid, high-pitched notes. Those lucky enough to hear this song may not ever manage to see the bird that is producing it.

The best place to spot a Nightingale is across the south-east of England, in Essex, Kent, Sussex and East Anglia.

LESSER SPOTTED WOODPECKER
Dendrocopos minor

The Lesser Spotted Woodpecker is the smallest of our three resident woodpeckers. It is a resident woodland bird, and much more conspicuous than the Nightingale or Cuckoo. The adult male has a distinctive red cap and white face. Its nape, back and wings are black with a white barred pattern across. The breast and underside is all white, which helps distinguish it from the larger Great Spotted Woodpecker, which has a white breast and red underside. Adult females are similar, except they have a black cap and no red below.

Lesser Spotted Woodpeckers inhabit mixed woodland, and spend much of their time high on tree trunks searching for insects. They have a shrill *pee-pee-pee-pee* song, and a short *kik* call. You may hear them drumming rapidly on trees; this drumming is rapid, much quicker than that of the Great Spotted Woodpecker.

Sightings of this woodpecker are rare, due to its decreasing population. This has been attributed partly to competition with larger woodpeckers for food. But the main culprit is almost certainly the destruction of ancient woodland through modern woodland management practices, including the removal of dead or rotting trees, which are crucial to the Lesser Spotted Woodpecker's feeding and breeding habits.

TREE PIPIT   *Anthus trivialis*

The adult Tree Pipit is light brown with darker streaks across the back and wings. These streaks darken from spring into summer. The head is also light brown with a pale band across the eye, and the bird has a cream-coloured throat and breast. There are streaks on the breast, which become finer on the flanks and underside. Juveniles look the same, although they are more yellow than cream.

Tree Pipits can be seen perching in bushes or walking along broad tree branches. They prefer woodland with open spaces beneath the canopy, and search for insects on the ground. They also flit between perches when singing, so it is best to look out for them where tree distribution is less dense – you will hear a high-pitched warbling song, or a buzzing *teeee* call if a Tree Pipit is nearby. These birds are summer visitors to Britain, and sadly there has been a marked decrease in their numbers over the past 25 years.

BIRDS OF PREY

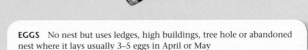

KESTREL *Falco tinnunculus*

The Kestrel is probably the most easily spotted of the native birds of prey. It is a fairly common sight hovering by roadside verges or perching on telegraph poles and phone wires, and can be recognized by its pointed wings and long tail. However, the intensification of farming methods has resulted in a decline in habitats and a corresponding decline in birds – despite the Kestrel's adaptability and its move into urban areas.

EGGS   No nest but uses ledges, high buildings, tree hole or abandoned nest where it lays usually 3–5 eggs in April or May

SONG   High-pitched, rapid *kee-kee-kee-kee* call; not usually heard unless birds are 'playing ' together or the male is chasing the female in courtship

DIET   Small mammals, frogs, worms and insects; birds living in towns take small birds

HABITAT   Many habitats, from woodland to heath, farmland to urban areas; does not favour dense forests, treeless wetlands or mountains

HOBBY *Falco subbuteo*

Although not a UK resident, the Hobby arrives to breed in April, leaving around September or October. A similar size to a Kestrel, Hobbies have striped underparts and long pointed wings, and are sometimes mistaken for a giant Swallow. Hobbies hunt down insects in flight, usually snatching their prey from the air then transferring it from claw to beak in mid-flight.

Their aerobatics are most noticeable in courtship when male and female circle together in long soaring flight during which the male stoops (collapses its wings to travel at great speed like an arrow) on the female as if to attack her. These birds take such delight in their acrobatics, it is widely thought that they fly for fun.

EGGS   Usually lays 3 eggs in June

SONG   Chirruping *kwee-kwee-kwee* call

DIET   Grasshoppers, dragonflies and other winged insects, small birds, and occasionally bats

HABITAT   Usually around woodland edges, and heathland

GOSHAWK *Accipiter gentilis*

Persecution rendered Goshawks extinct in the nineteenth century and it ceased to feature in bird books. Migrant birds and falconers' escapees have seen its reintroduction and there are now an estimated 400-plus pairs resident throughout the country.

Female

Almost as big as a Buzzard, the Goshawk has a fierce expression, owing to its distinctive red eyes and white 'eyebrow'. It will aggressively defend its nest and eggs from all potential adversaries, even humans. Broad wings enable it to weave in and out of trees when hunting, and long legs and talons mean it can catch its quarry in flight.

Goshawks are secretive, and the best time to see them is during the breeding season or in autumn.

Male

At this time of year the male displays in flight, its movements forming what can be best described as a rollercoaster over the trees.

EGGS   Nests in April and lays 3–4 eggs in May

SONG   Classic falcon call of *kweeeeeeee-kweeeeeeee-kweeeee-kik-kik-kik-kik*

DIET   Small woodland mammals and birds such as pigeon, dove, crow and partridge

HABITAT   Large woods and forests with glades and paths along which it hunts; also seen hunting in open countryside

SPARROWHAWK *Accipiter nisus*

Male Sparrowhawks are distinguishable by their slate grey back and white underparts which show close orange bars. Females are larger, brown and have a white stripe over the eye. The bird's short, rounded wings make it ideally designed for flying closely around its dense layered hunting grounds.

The Sparrowhawk relies on its speed when hunting, making a surprise attack. It will skim along one side of a hedgerow, before flitting over it, surprising a flock of finches and taking one in flight. If it fails in this enterprise it will not try again, preferring to fly off and seek a new hunting ground.

EGGS   4–6 eggs usually laid in late May

SONG   High-pitched rapid *chit-chit-chit-chit-chit-chit-chit* or *kek-kek-kek-kek* followed be a long *weeow-weeow*

DIET   Mainly small birds. Occasionally mice, voles, young rabbits and insects

HABITAT   Mostly found in woodland and hedgerows across the UK, sometimes in parks and gardens. Usually sighted flying low and fast while in the pursuit of quarry

BIRDS OF PREY

TAWNY OWL *Strix aluco*

About the size of a pigeon, the Tawny Owl is the country's most widespread breeding species, although it is not found in Ireland. It has a ring of brown feathers atop a rounded body, with a reddish brown back and paler underparts. Tawny Owls can sometimes be seen at roost during the day. Look for pellets of undigested material on the ground and then look up to the branches of the nearest trees where they may be seen leaning against the trunk.

EGGS Lays 2–4 eggs between March and May, sometimes earlier, in a hole in a tree or an old squirrel drey

SONG *Kee-wick, hoo, hoo, hoo-oo-oo-oo*. A common misconception is that this is the call of one owl when in reality it is two owls calling each other

DIET Small mammals, rodents, birds, frogs, fish, insects and worms

HABITAT Mainly woodland and some urban areas. Can usually be heard calling at night, but it is very difficult to see

LITTLE OWL *Athene noctua*

Introduced to Kent and Northamptonshire at the end of the 1800s, the Little Owl spread rapidly across Britain. It is probably the easiest of the owls to spot. When it is hunting at dawn and dusk, it can be seen perching on telegraph poles and fence posts or in a tree. In flight is can be distinguished by its undulating course on long, rounded wings which produce rapid beats. When disturbed, it bobs its head up and down in alarm.

Originally thought by gamekeepers to be responsible for a decline in game stocks, the Little Owl actually eats the leather-jacket larvae of the crane-fly, a notorious farmland pest, and now enjoys the same protection as native owls.

EGGS Nests in a hole in a tree or wall using no nesting materials and lays 3–5 eggs in late April to early May

SONG Rapid *kwee-kwee-kwee-kwee-kwee* followed by a long *ieou-ieou-ieou*

DIET Small mammals, birds, beetles and worms; also earwigs, other insects and frogs

HABITAT Lowland farmland with hedges and copses, sometimes parks and orchards

Barn Owl Tyto alba

The Barn Owl is a much-loved member of the countryside. It has a heart-shaped face, buff back and wings with either white or speckled underparts. Sexes can be distinguished by the spots on the underside of their wings: males have tiny, or no, spots whereas females have clearly defined spots.

The Barn Owl hunts mostly at dawn or dusk. It is silent in flight owing to the configuration of its primary feathers, which allow air to flow over them without displacement. Its hearing is as important as its acute eyesight, with its face acting as a satellite dish to pick up the slightest disturbance heard with its asymmetrically placed ears.

Over the past few decades the Barn Owl population has declined owing to changes in farming practices and the degradation of prey-rich habitats and breeding sites. However, recently a reversal in these practices, along with a licensed scheme allowing for the introduction of captive-bred birds, has contributed to the increase in the wild population.

EGGS   Clutch sizes of typically 4–6 eggs depending on habitat

SONG   A distinctive screeching call

DIET   Mice, voles and shrews

HABITAT   Open country, along field edges, riverbanks and roadside verges

Long-eared Owl Asio otus

The Long-eared Owl is no bigger than a wood pigeon. Its 'ears' are not used for hearing as they are tufts of head feathers. Their function is as a sign that the bird is alarmed, when it raises them in order to appear larger than it is.

Despite being reclusive, the male has a particular courtship flight, clapping its wings together and then jumping in the air.

The best chance of sighting this owl is when it is roosting on a favourite branch, leaning against the trunk, or when it is in flight during migration. When roosting, its presence may be given away by the pellets on the ground below its branch, or by the angry mob of smaller birds (on which it feeds) trying to scare it away: listen for a hissing cry and beak snapping which the bird uses as a warning display.

EGGS   Usually uses nest left by members of the crow family or a squirrel's drey, laying 4–5 eggs around March or April

SONG   A staccato *hoo-hoo-hoo* which sounds as if it's calling into a tin can

DIET   Small rodents: mice, rats, voles and shrews. In winter will feed on small birds, occasionally taking prey as large as a Jay or Magpie

HABITAT   Woodland areas up to the edges of open countryside

GRASSLAND, MOOR AND MOUNTAIN BIRDS

For many of us, a grassy hill in the open countryside and the diminishing trill of the Skylark's song as it slowly rises into the air, makes a leisurely walk all the more special. But there are other birds that enjoy open countryside, and that we can enjoy as we explore such landscapes. Read further and you can find out about the Red Grouse, the Fieldfare and the Whinchat – and many more of our beloved birds.

THE GRASSLAND, MOOR AND MOUNTAIN HABITAT

Moors offer little scope to the farmer and so have not been developed in the past. This has made moors a useful habitat for birds such as Skylarks, Nightjars, Linnets and Wheatears, which all appreciate an open countryside far from humans. In the twenty-first century, though, some of this land is being lost to housing developments and to recreational purposes such as off-road driving. Where this occurs, birds inevitably lose their breeding and feeding grounds. Stonechats and rare Warblers have so far been identified as suffering from this loss of habitat.

In upland areas, such as the Scottish Highlands, birds are doing well due to concerted conservation efforts. More Golden Eagles and Peregrine Falcons have been breeding successfully in these areas than before. However, one issue is the loss of heather land due to grazing, mainly by sheep, which is affecting rare species of Grouse.

Most grassland has been developed and maintained for farming purposes. Once, farm pastures offered an ideal habitat – abundant seeds, shoots and insect life – for many species of bird. The picture nowadays is not so rosy. What to the farmer is improved grazing – fast-growing, non-native grass species managed with selective herbicides – is of little use to birds. Other farmland has its problems too. For example, arable fields once provided food for many species of bird, but modern intensive farming too often means a loss of opportunity. Seeds from arable crops are harvested so effectively that there is little left for bird life; wild seeds are wiped out through the use of herbicides; and insecticides kill off the minibeasts that birds feed on. As a result, numbers of many birds, such as the Grey Partridge, Bunting and Yellow Wagtail, are in decline.

However, farmland does still provide many opportunities for birds, despite the problems outlined above. In times of freezing weather or drought, birds will visit animal troughs for water to drink. Also, in periods of severe weather, many species congregate around outbuildings where they hope to find spillages of animal feed, and the warmth of housed animals. Blackbirds and Song Thrushes, normally very territorial, will travel far outside their normal ranges to freshly tilled fields to feed, and Twite, a moorland bird, can often be found on farmland borders to make use of food supplies there. Farming produces seasonal opportunities

for birds also: groups of Rooks and Gulls can often be seen squabbling over freshly dug ground as they follow ploughs through the fields.

Adapting to changes in habitat

Birds adapt in various ways to loss of, and changes to, their natural environment. Moor and grassland habitats are becoming important to species of birds normally found in other habitats. Curlews and Lapwings, for example, are wading birds that have adapted to breeding and resting in these types of habitats, as their estuarine sites have become over-developed.

Over-intensive grouse hunting has meant that Merlins and other birds of prey are making the shift from feeding on Grouse and small animals to House Sparrows, while Kestrel and Barn Owl have seen numbers rise in the farmland areas they favour for hunting.

Other birds are adapting by using heathland not frequented by humans. For example, some birds now use military training areas for breeding purposes. In fact, some of these areas have now become official conservation zones.

Conservation efforts

As many bird species have come close to extinction, conservationists have responded with strategies to help birds living in moorland, grassland and mountain habitats regain a foothold. Unfortunately, some of these efforts have met opposition from farmers and gamekeepers. For example, the reintroduction of the Golden Eagle has met with hostility as the birds are accused of feeding on newborn lambs. This has resulted in Eagles being poisoned, although this is highly illegal.

Studies show that a reduction in foxes and Crows leads to a subsequent increase in numbers of Lapwing, Curlew, Golden Plover, Red Grouse and Meadow Pipit. Pest management is one, possibly controversial, tool in the toolkit of conservationists who are attempting to improve the numbers of such bird species.

One remarkable development is the reintroduction of the Great Bustard, one of the world's heaviest flying birds, last seen in the British Isles in the 1840s. Their extinction was largely due to changes in farmland management and trophy hunting, but they are now breeding successfully on Salisbury Plain.

DIPPER   *Cinclus cinclus*

ADULT   At first glance, the Dipper could pass for an overgrown wren. Both sexes have a dark grey back contrasting with a startlingly white chest, which disappears into a broad, bright chestnut girdle round the belly. The rich brown head sports a sturdy dark beak, and the black legs are strong and thick, ending in suitably large feet. In fact, this engaging bird is fairly solid altogether, its chunky body easily identified in the sky.

JUVENILE   Young birds are a lighter grey with pale edging on the feathers.

EGGS   The neat, domed nest made from grass, leaves and moss is normally tucked into a convenient hole in the bank of a river or reservoir. It may alternatively be hidden behind a waterfall, in a rock crevice, or suspended from an overhanging tree or bridge. Females lay two broods of pure white eggs between April and July.

SONG   With its piercing loud *dzitz*, the Dipper's voice is difficult to ignore. Its song, however, is slightly more melodic, being a deep, rich warble punctuated by grating, earsplitting sounds.

LENGTH	18 cm (7 in)
WINGSPAN	25–30 cm (10–12 in)
BREEDING STARTS	April
NUMBER OF EGGS PER CLUTCH	4–6

J	
F	
M	
A	
M	
J	
J	
A	
S	
O	
N	
D	

Where in UK Dippers can be seen

Months when Dippers can be seen

DIET   Living by water means a varied diet for the Dipper. Small fish, aquatic insects and their larvae, molluscs and snails are all on the menu, yet each requires a different way of being caught. Uniquely, Dippers will walk, swim, dive or wade in pursuit of individual prey.

HABITAT   Dippers can be seen all year round, wherever there's a fast-flowing river or freshwater lake in moorland, tree-lined valleys and ravines. In the winter, some birds may head for a larger body of water such as reservoirs, but they tend to remain inland.

OTHER   The bird's flight is fast and low, with flurries of wingbeats as it races up and down the water's edge. Another name for the Dipper is Water Ouzel.

FIELDFARE *Turdus pilaris*

ADULT The Fieldfare is a common winter visitor. This rather majestic-looking bird is a member of the thrush family, and has a colour scheme not unlike that of the Song Thrush, with a chestnut-brown upper and a magnificent gold-buff breast generously flecked with black. The blue-grey head has a pale mask around the eyes and the beak is black and yellow. The sexes are alike. In flight, the Fieldfare flashes its white underwings. During the winter months its flanks are white and the rump turns to grey.

JUVENILE Although juvenile males and females are like each other, they can be distinguished from adults by pale brown spots on their wing coverts.

EGGS Only small numbers of Fieldfares breed in this country. Where this occurs, they lay blue-green eggs in cuplike nests of twigs, fibres and rootlets in trees.

SONG The song is a distinctive, but unmelodic, nasal *chak-chak-chak* sound that varies in pitch and volume and incorporates an unappealing range of warbles, shrieks and whistling.

DIET Food is mainly worms and insects, which are eaten on the ground, but the bird also eats fruit such as berries and apples whenever these can be found.

HABITAT The birds arrive in flocks in October and generally leave about April. While here, they inhabit open heathland and fields, or the edges of woods. Their favourite haunts are old orchards and meadows, especially those lined with hedges and trees.

LENGTH	24–26 cm (9½–10½ in)
WINGSPAN	39–42 cm (15–16½ in)
BREEDING STARTS	May
NUMBER OF EGGS PER CLUTCH	5–6

Where in UK
Fieldfares
can be seen

Months when
Fieldfares
can be seen

OTHER These handsome creatures are very sociable. They move around and feed together, and can often be seen with other species such as Redwings and Blackbirds. Flocks of Fieldfares are a fine sight: their flight is undulating and rather strong, and has a repertoire of glides interspersed by furious wing beats.

GREY PARTRIDGE *Perdix perdix*

ADULT Despite its name, the Grey Partridge is actually quite colourful, with its light-orange face and intricately patterned brown and grey plumage. The bird has a small, neat head, brown bill, streaky back, a grey-streaked breast and striking chestnut bars on each side of its rotund body. Both sexes have a dark brown patch on the belly, which is larger in the male. In flight, the tail fans open to display a warm orange, and the pale wings are slightly curved and fingered.

JUVENILE Immature birds are sandy-coloured with buff streaks.

EGGS Grey Partridges live on the ground and their nests are shallow scrapes furnished with leaves and grass and sheltered by the tall swaying grasses of arable land. Although there is only one brood per year, the hen can lay as many as 20 eggs.

SONG The voice is creaky and rhythmic, a low *chirrick* or *kieerk*.

DIET Grey Partridges feed on seeds, leaves, caterpillars and insects, picking them up as they move cautiously through meadows and pastures. They will also eat green shoots. The Partridge feeds its chicks with insects, which have become less freely available of recent years, due to increased use of pesticides and herbicides. This has, in turn, had an effect on the adult population.

LENGTH	29–31 cm (11½–12 in)
WINGSPAN	45–48 cm (18–19 in)
BREEDING STARTS	April
NUMBER OF EGGS PER CLUTCH	10–20

J
F
M
A
M
J
J
A
S
O
N
D

Where in UK Grey Partridges can be seen

Months when Grey Partridges can be seen

HABITAT The Grey Partridge is generally seen in open grassland, heathland and farmland, especially that with mature hedgerows. Because of its status as a game bird, and the threat to its chicks as mentioned above, numbers have declined dramatically over recent decades.

OTHER Where the bird does exist, families of them collect together in flocks or 'coveys' which, when disturbed, will fly off as one, their arched wings beating rapidly between intermittent glides.

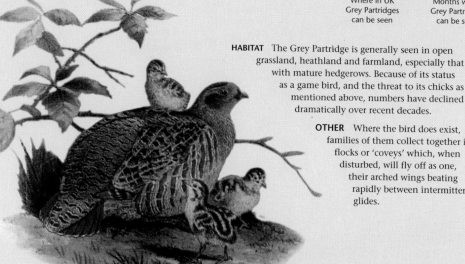

RED GROUSE *Lagopus lagopus scoticus*

ADULT The Red Grouse is a stocky, medium-sized, plump-bodied game bird. A little smaller than other grouse varieties, it has sturdy white-feathered legs, dark-brown wings and a short bill with a slightly hooked tip. The male's upper and lower body is an all-over rich chestnut brown while the smaller female is a less colourful speckled brown-grey. Both sexes sport a red wattle above the eyes and, again, this is duller and less pronounced in the female.

JUVENILE Juveniles do not have wattles or combs and are the same dun colour as their mother. Notably precocious, they start to feed themselves on a diet of insects soon after hatching, and they are able to fly at 13 days, when only half-grown.

EGGS Females lay greyish-white eggs, camouflaged with grey-brown speckles. These are incubated for around 3 weeks in a shallow nest scrape, concealed by heather and bilberry. For a short time after hatching, both males and females care for the young.

SONG The Red Grouse's song is harsh and unmelodious, a cackling *go-back-go-back* caw which is most aggressive when the male is marking out its territory.

DIET They are essentially herbivorous, using their tough beaks on seeds, berries, cereals and insects, although they can enjoy the occasional snail.

HABITAT Red Grouse can be seen all year round. They inhabit uplands, moorland and heather tundra where they can go undetected. They don't travel far and, once they find the ideal territory, tend to stay put regardless of the season.

LENGTH	33–42 cm (13–16 in)
WINGSPAN	55–66 cm (22–27 in)
BREEDING STARTS	April
NUMBER OF EGGS PER CLUTCH	6–8

Where in UK Red Grouse can be seen

Months when Red Grouse can be seen

OTHER If you disturb a Red Grouse, you will know about it. Take-off is sudden and dramatic and the bird's low flight away from the intruder is aided by short round wings, which whir rapidly then occasionally pause as the bird does a short glide.

LINNET *Carduelis cannabina*

ADULT In the summer, the male Linnet has a plain orangey-brown upper, a red breast and a pale fawn head capped with a bright crimson brow that grows darker in spring – as does the rest of its plumage. The wings are brown with faint white markings. Both sexes have a sharp grey bill and pale cheek spots, and the female is duller and much browner than the male, with a tawny-buff breast and white belly. In winter, there is little to tell them apart as the male loses his rose-coloured chest and changes to a dark, streaky grey-brown like his mate.

JUVENILE With their brown plumage, juveniles are similar to the females but paler with bold streaks. There is a faint yellow tinge on their otherwise pale grey legs and bill.

EGGS Breeding is from April to July, giving the Linnet time to nurture two or even three broods. Built from stems and roots and lined with hair, the nests are small but meticulously tidy. They are usually found in bushes or hedgerows, which offer plenty of protection for the blue-green eggs with rust-coloured speckles.

SONG Linnets are famed for their rich, melodic song, which varies between twitters and chatters in flight. Otherwise, the birds warble and chatter intermittently, with the occasional tuneful chorus from the rest of the flock. At times, Linnet song has been compared to that of the Canary, although the Linnet has a wider range and is actually more musical.

LENGTH	12.5–14 cm (5–5½ in)
WINGSPAN	21–25 cm (8½–10 in)
BREEDING STARTS	April
NUMBER OF EGGS PER CLUTCH	4–6

Where in UK Linnets can be seen

Months when Linnets can be seen

DIET The basic diet is seed pecked from the ground by colonies of birds who feed together all year round. The juveniles are fed on insects until they fledge.

HABITAT Linnets can easily be found almost everywhere in the UK except north-west Scotland and uplands, their favourite habitats being heaths, scrub, salt marshes, farm hedges and commons. They rarely, if ever, visit gardens as they tend to be nervous and intensely shy of humans.

OTHER When flying, Linnets can be as tidy as their nests, coordinating their movements so the whole flock dips and soars, dancing on the air while beating their wings in perfect unison. Linnets were popular pets in the nineteenth and early twentieth centuries, as they were loved for their cheery, tuneful singing.

GOLDEN PLOVER   *Pluvialis apricania*

ADULT The summer plumage of the Golden Plover is strikingly beautiful. Gold-, black- and white-beaded plumage on the upper body contrasts with a shiny black breast and belly fringed with a broad white border. Both sexes are broadly similar. The plumage changes quite dramatically in winter; the belly turns white and the breast becomes lighter with a faint yellow blush. The upper parts now have a dark brown base spangled with yellow, while the rump is a dense brown, giving an overall effect that is subtler but no less attractive. White underwings are displayed during flight and there is a white bar on the upper wing.

JUVENILE Immature birds have similar colouring to the adult in winter and grow to have the same long grey legs and stubby beak.

EGGS In spring and early summer, the female lays a single clutch of blotched buff eggs in a shallow scrape on moorland or grass. Areas with burnt bracken are also favoured; here nests are lined with lichen and heather.

SONG The song when on the ground is a plaintive flute-like whistle, interspersed by high-pitched variants of *tlooee*; the song-flight is distinguished by a series of *pheeoos* as flocks of plovers soar to great heights, forming into long rows or packs.

LENGTH	26–29 cm (10–11½ in)
WINGSPAN	67–76 cm (26–20 in)
BREEDING STARTS	April
NUMBER OF EGGS PER CLUTCH	4

Where in UK Golden Plover can be seen	Months when Golden Plover can be seen

DIET The Golden Plover enjoys a variety of insects in the summer, feeding in evenly spread flocks along the ground. Its diet changes to earthworms in the winter – however, there is plenty of competition from gulls which, ever the opportunists, will steal worms given the chance.

HABITAT Golden Plovers can be seen all year round in the UK, mostly on northern moorland hills and limestone grasslands. When the weather turns cold, they are also spotted in lower-lying farmland, salt marshes near the coast and estuaries.

OTHER Flocks of these birds are usually fairly loose but, if threatened or roosting, the birds gather together tightly for protection.

RING OUZEL *Turdus torquatus*

ADULT The Ring Ouzel is a relative of the Blackbird, and can be said to replace it in the upland parts of the UK. Males are almost black except for a yellow beak, broad white crescent on the breast and a brownish-charcoal back. This medium-sized bird strikes quite an attitude – holding its head high and cocking its long sooty tail. In flight, the wings are pale in contrast to the dense black underside. Females are slimmer, with smaller heads, muted, speckled plumage and a pale, dull breast band, which may be indistinct.

JUVENILE In juveniles, the breast band or bib is absent altogether and the feathers are brown with a scaly effect.

EGGS In spring and early summer, the female produces two broods, cosseted in a large, cup-like nest loosely made from twigs, leaves, grass and other vegetation. Typical breeding sites include rock crevices, dilapidated dry stone walls and steep banks on the rocky moors or upper ground.

SONG The voice is a loud, repetitive *tchak-tchak* mixed in with chuckling and chattering, whereas the song is a more melodic, fluting *tchoo-tchoo*.

LENGTH	23–24 cm (9–9½ in)
WINGSPAN	38–42 cm (15–16½ in)
BREEDING STARTS	April
NUMBER OF EGGS PER CLUTCH	5–6

J
F
M
A
M
J
J
A
S
O
N
D

Where in UK
Ring Ouzels
can be seen

Months when
Ring Ouzels
can be seen

Female

Male

Juvenile

DIET Seeds, insects and worms are the basic diet of Ring Ouzels, though they also take berries, especially during migration when they can be seen snatching the fruit from bushes in passing.

HABITAT Ring Ouzels are present in the UK from March to November, most commonly on windswept bracken hills, craggy moors, gullies and peat bogs. In early spring and late autumn, they can occasionally be spotted on coasts and cliffs.

OTHER These birds are shyer than other thrushes, which makes them hard to spot. Recently, populations have declined, and they are considered to be a species at risk.

ROOK *Corvus frugilegus*

ADULT Rook females and males are alike. They have glossy, ink-black wings and body, and the feathers on the thighs are rather untidy, like a pair of ragged cut-off denims. The head is 'interesting' rather than handsome, with a pointed crown and long tapering bill encased by bare white skin around the base. The Rook is very similar to the Carrion Crow, the main differences being the wings, which are more pointed in the Rook, and the tail – the Rook's being thinner and rounded.

JUVENILE Juveniles are virtually smaller versions of the adults, but the face is darker and the bill finer.

EGGS Although it has been known for a couple of pairs to isolate themselves, Rooks normally breed in colonies, building their large stick nests in tall trees where they are clearly visible until the summer when everything is in leaf. The nests are lined with moss, grass and straw, and provide a safe home for the eggs (which are olive-green with brown spots) and later for the nestlings.

DIET Favourite feeding areas include ploughed fields, where birds will pluck out roots and seeds to supplement their diet of larvae, worms and other invertebrates. They also scavenge along roadsides for roadkill such as hares or rabbits.

LENGTH	44–46 cm (17½–18 in)
WINGSPAN	81–99 cm (32–39 in)
BREEDING STARTS	March
NUMBER OF EGGS PER CLUTCH	3–6

Where in UK Rooks can be seen

Months when Rooks can be seen

Adult

Juvenile

HABITAT Present in the UK all year, Rooks are typically seen in farmland, parks and spacious gardens where there are tall trees for nesting. This large crow is extremely sociable, not just towards its own species but also to Stock Doves and certain types of gull.

OTHER Rooks are hard to miss, producing as they do a cacophony of loud, raucous cawing. Flight is strong, steady and often soaring, but these large birds are nimble too, twisting and swooping around the colony.

PIED WAGTAIL   *Motacilla alba*

ADULT In summer, the male Pied Wagtail has attractive pied plumage, with a black back, black underside, black wings, dark flanks and a black head with a white face and charcoal beak. The female is just as eye-catching, but lighter than the male and has a greyer back. When in flight the male displays distinctive white streaks and narrow bars on its wings which separate at the tip into finger feathers.

JUVENILE In juveniles, the white face has yet to appear and the body is virtually grey all over apart from a buff underside.

EGGS Eggs are pale grey, smooth and glossy, with dark grey spots. They are laid in two or three separate broods. The cup-like nests are made from grass and can be found in all sorts of unusual places – banks, cliffs, log piles, barns and shed, and even under bridges.

SONG The song is a mixture of highly tuneful chirrups and trills, morphing into harsher *tziks tsiks* as the birds gather together.

DIET Their food consists of insects, flies and seeds taken from the ground, from roadsides or pavements, or from roofs. The bird also takes molluscs from the waterside.

HABITAT A charming little bird, the pied wagtail is welcome everywhere and will live almost anywhere. Pied wagtails can be seen all year round and are as likely to be found in city centres or industrial estates as in grassland, farmland and by remote rivers or cliffs. Strangely though, the one place they are rarely spotted is in a typical country garden.

OTHER Pied Wagtails sometimes form communes in shopping centres and even factories, as long as there are trees to shelter in and provide food. In fact, urban areas provide rich pickings for the birds.

LENGTH	18 cm (7 in)
WINGSPAN	25–30 cm (10–12 in)
BREEDING STARTS	April
NUMBER OF EGGS PER CLUTCH	3–6 (2–3 broods)

J
F
M
A
M
J
J
A
S
O
N
D

Where in UK
Pied Wagtails
can be seen

Months when
Pied Wagtails
can be seen

SKYLARK   *Alauda arvensis*

ADULT   When the Skylark is on the ground, it is hard to spot. This brown bird with streaky black markings is scarcely bigger than a Sparrow, its only distinguishing feature being a small head crest which rises with excitement or alarm. The tail and wings are fringed in white, and it has plump, yellowy legs and a buff-coloured belly. Males and females look exactly alike.

JUVENILE   Juveniles are like the adults, but their feathers have a pale edge to them, which give them a scaly look.

EGGS   The Skylark lays shiny grey-tinged eggs with brown and yellow spots in cup-sized nests made from grass and hair. It has the shortest incubation period of any other UK bird – just 11 days. The female keeps the nest warm, then both parents feed the chicks until they are fully fledged at 20 days.

SONG   Despite its tiny size, the Skylark has the most impressive flight song, rising vertically to a tremendous height. Here it hangs with fluttering wings, filling the air with continuous, vibrant melody before plummeting back to earth.

DIET   The Skylark eats seeds, grain and insects. In spring and early summer it may also eat the new shoots of field crops or of grass.

HABITAT   Skylarks prefer open country such as downland, gorse-covered moorland or pasture, but can be seen anywhere in Britain which offers the right terrain. In winter, some birds seek a lower, warmer environment.

LENGTH	18–19 cm (7½ in)
WINGSPAN	30–36 cm (12–14 in)
BREEDING STARTS	April
NUMBER OF EGGS PER CLUTCH	3–5

Where in UK Skylarks can be seen

Months when Skylarks can be seen

OTHER   Skylarks never land on bushes or trees, but always on the ground. Because of their speckled plumage, they can be hard to see, blending perfectly with their surroundings. But it is in the air where they seem completely at home, their liquid chirrup brightening up the day. Sadly, the Skylark's numbers are dwindling, as a result of changes in farming practices.

YELLOW WAGTAIL *Motacilla flava*

ADULT With its eye-catching plumage and graceful shape, the Yellow Wagtail is a welcome summer visitor. Its bright colour is strongly evident during the spring, both in its canary-yellow underparts and racy eye stripe. The olive-green upper and crown contrast with the breast and belly, while the tail is edged in white. The head is neat with a dark cheek patch and a sharp beak curving slightly downwards, and its charcoal wings display two narrow bars in flight. Females are lighter with a greeny-grey back and pale eye stripe, but both sexes are duller in winter.

JUVENILE Immature birds are similar to the female but with white-lined wings, and the underside is buff with a hint of yellow on the tail.

EGGS The Wagtail constructs grassy cup-like nests on the ground, which it lines with hair; it chooses spots where the nests can be protected by surrounding vegetation. Dappled white and grey eggs are then laid in two broods.

SONG The best way to distinguish this bird from other wagtails is by its full-throated *tsik, tsueep* and intermittent musical chirping.

DIET Yellow Wagtails can be found close to grazing livestock, because these animals attract flies, which are a useful source of protein for the bird. The birds skip along the ground in groups, snatching flies, insects and various tidbits as they go.

LENGTH	17 cm (7 in)
WINGSPAN	23–27 cm (9–10½ in)
BREEDING STARTS	May
NUMBER OF EGGS PER CLUTCH	5–6 (2 broods)

| J |
| F |
| M |
| A |
| M |
| J |
| J |
| A |
| S |
| O |
| N |
| D |

Where in UK
Yellow Wagtails
can be seen

Months when
Yellow Wagtails
can be seen

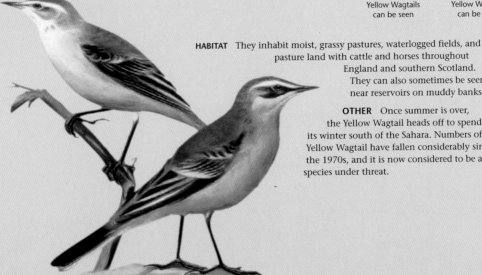

HABITAT They inhabit moist, grassy pastures, waterlogged fields, and pasture land with cattle and horses throughout England and southern Scotland. They can also sometimes be seen near reservoirs on muddy banks.

OTHER Once summer is over, the Yellow Wagtail heads off to spend its winter south of the Sahara. Numbers of Yellow Wagtail have fallen considerably since the 1970s, and it is now considered to be a species under threat.

STONECHAT *Saxicola torquata*

ADULT A stocky little bird, the male Stonechat can be identified by the white patch on each side of the neck, which is in stark contrast to the blackish head, throat and upper. The lower body has a rusty red breast that fades to a pale fawn belly and is supported by slender black legs. There is a pale V-shaped rump tapering to a short black tail, and a large white patch on both upper wings close to the body is clearly visible in flight. The female has a similar appearance but a paler head and throat.

JUVENILE Young birds can be distinguished from adults by their heavily mottled chests. They have a pale head and throat, like the female.

EGGS There are usually two broods of blue-green eggs, finely speckled with brown. These are laid in cup-shaped nests of grass, lined with feathers and hair and accessed through a purpose-built tunnel.

SONG The Stonechat's song is rather harsh and grating, a *tjak-tjak* intermingled with an equally strident *whee-tak-tak*. In flight, the song is fast, chattery and not very musical.

DIET Stonechats eat insects, spiders, worm and seeds. In some areas they are appreciated for keeping down the insects and maggots that sheep harbour in their wool.

HABITAT Stonechats are fairly easily spotted at any time of year in windswept areas of the British Isles. They favour moorland, heaths, conifer plantations and scrub during the breeding season; in the winter they may also be found on cliffs around the coast.

LENGTH	12.5–14 cm (5–5½ in)
WINGSPAN	21–25 cm (8½–10 in)
BREEDING STARTS	April
NUMBER OF EGGS PER CLUTCH	4–6

Where in UK
Stonechats
can be seen

Months when
Stonechats
can be seen

Adult

Female

OTHER You may see a Stonechat sitting on its lookout – a thicket of gorse, a hawthorn bush or an overhead telephone or electricity line – with tail flicking, waiting for its favourite food. When the bird spots something to eat it drops to the ground, and takes its food back to the perch to be eaten. Or you may spot it flying low, heading quickly and unceremoniously for the next convenient perch.

TWITE *Carduelis flavirostris*

ADULT The male Twite has dark brown stripes on its tawny back and grey-buff breast which fades to white on the belly. There are no markings on its pale tan face and throat. The beak is grey in summer, and yellow in the winter. When outstretched, the charcoal wings have attractive whitish streaks and pale thin bars. In flight, the male is colourful, displaying a rose-pink rump, particularly in the summer months during the breeding season. The female is similar in colouring to the winter male, though with a brown rump.

JUVENILE The juvenile is almost indistinguishable from the adult female.

EGGS The bird prefers treeless habitats for breeding, including stony areas on the coast, or upland heaths with bracken and gorse. It builds a deep cup-shaped nest from twigs, grass and hair, choosing a sheltered spot close to the ground, in a bush or shrub, or on a stone ledge or wall. The female lays one or two clutches of bluish-white eggs. Twites usually nest singly or in small colonies and will fly several kilometres to find food for their young.

SONG The song is a blend of rapid trills and tweets, sounding like *twite*. It is rather nasal in tone, with a distinctive twang. This song can be heard as the birds fly in flocks, rising, circling and dipping in unison, with wings flapping energetically.

DIET Twites are strictly herbivorous and live on a diet of seeds from various wild herbs and flowers including dandelions, sorrel and thistle. These are pecked daintily from the ground – the birds' preferred feeding place. Juveniles are virtually unique in that they are fed on seeds as soon as they are hatched.

LENGTH	12.5–14 cm (5–5½ in)
WINGSPAN	21–25 cm (8½–10 in)
BREEDING STARTS	May
NUMBER OF EGGS PER CLUTCH	4–6

Where in UK Twites can be seen

Months when Twites can be seen

HABITAT Although found on moorland during the summer, Twites tend to winter in open places, usually on shores and salt marshes around the coast.

OTHER Outside the breeding season, Twites sometimes form large flocks, either of the one species or mixed with other finches.

WHEATEAR   *Oenanthe oenanthe*

ADULT   The Wheatear is a delicate little bird. Males have a pale-grey upper and an undercarriage blushed with peach which goes browner in the autumn. Its large, white, V-shaped rump is conspicuous in flight, contrasting with dark wings, black tail bands and black ear coverts, and the Wheatear also sports a dashing black eye patch. Although females have similar markings, their undercarriage is a plainer buff and the eye patch is brown, colouring mirrored by their young but with speckled feathers.

JUVENILE   The juvenile Wheatear has greyish-brown upper parts, a pale belly, and an orangey-buff throat, face and flanks.

EGGS   Females lay pale greeny-blue eggs with light brown flecks, incubating them in crudely built nests of grass and weeds under clumps of earth or stones. Occasionally the bird chooses to nest in a disused rabbit burrow or a hollow in a dry stone wall. The eggs have a 14-day incubation period and the chicks are independent after 30 days. Sometimes, Wheatears will have a second clutch.

SONG   The Wheatear has a sharp alarm call: *chak*, like two stones banged together. The song is a sharp, cheerful and rather disjointed warble.

LENGTH	14–16 cm (5½–6½ in)
WINGSPAN	29 cm (11 in)
BREEDING STARTS	April or May
NUMBER OF EGGS PER CLUTCH	3–6

J
F
M
A
M
J
J
A
S
O
N
D

Where in UK
Wheatears
can be seen

Months when
Wheatears
can be seen

DIET   The birds' diet consists of insects, grubs and other pests. This makes the birds popular with farmers in arable areas.

HABITAT   The best time to see this delightful little bird is spring to autumn. Their favoured habitats are open areas of moorland, heath or grassland where there is little vegetation.

OTHER   Once categorized as a thrush, the Wheatear has now been identified as a member of the flycatcher family, Muscicapidae. Males are possessive, guarding their mates to stop them breeding with rivals. In mid-October, Wheatears travel southwards for the winter, crossing oceans, icy wastes and searing deserts to reach their destination in North Africa. Incidentally, the name Wheatear is derived from the original term 'white arse', due to its shapely white rump!

WHINCHAT *Saxicola ribetra*

ADULT In spring, the Whinchat looks very similar to its relative the Stonechat. Both have a flecked tail and wings, and orangey underparts. However, the upper body is lighter in the autumn, paling on the back to a straw colour with black streaks. The main feature to look for is the white eye stripe on each side of the head, which is absent in the Stonechat. In spring and summer, the apricot breast of the male is more vivid, while the cheeks turn a dark charcoal. As usual, the female is less colourful, with streaks to the buff upper body, but she still has the white stripe over the eye, along with a striped cap and cheek. In flight, females have a white V-shape on either side of the tail.

JUVENILE Juveniles also have the distinctive stripe on the head, and their underside is a light muted yellow.

EGGS Whinchats lay one or two broods of greenish-blue eggs in nests of grass built low into a bush or heather.

SONG Characterized by *tuc-tucs* and *wheets*, the Whinchat's song is a series of loud, high-pitched whistles with rattles, trills and clicks thrown in.

DIET Insects and worms are the mainstay of the Whinchat diet, although it also eats berries and seeds. Having spotted something edible, the bird drops to the ground, picks up its prey and flies back to its perch to enjoy it.

LENGTH	12.5 cm (5 in)
WINGSPAN	21–24 cm (8½–9½ in)
BREEDING STARTS	May
NUMBER OF EGGS PER CLUTCH	5–6

Where in UK Whinchats can be seen

Months when Whinchats can be seen

Male

HABITAT From April to October, Whinchats can be seen in open spaces such as moors and grassland, where they may be spotted perching on tall stems or saplings. They spend winter near coastal regions in marshy or grassy areas.

OTHER The bird's flight is fairly rapid and flitting as the bird heads for somewhere narrow to perch, such as a fence or overhead cable.

Female

LESS COMMON BIRDS

RAVEN *Corvus corax*

The Raven's plumage can easily be described: black back, black underside, black beak, black wings, black legs. The world's biggest crow, it can actually look extremely menacing, especially when the feathers are raised around its head and throat, resulting in an impressive beard, thick neck and enlarged crown. Its thick, curved bill is unusually long, even for the bird's enormous head. With its sweeping diamond-shaped tail and broad wings with fingered, tapering feathers, the Raven is most impressive in flight as it soars effortlessly above the highest peaks.

Favourite haunts are forests, craggy hills, open moorland and mountains in upland areas of the west and south-west. In the south-east, the only place to see Ravens is at the Tower of London. Due to a long-held superstition that England will fall if the Ravens leave the tower, their wings are clipped to prevent them doing so.

PTARMIGAN *Lagopus mutus*

The Ptarmigan is a bantam-shaped grouse. In summer, the male Ptarmigan has striking grey and white upper plumage, contrasting with his pure white underside and thickly feathered white legs. He can also be distinguished by a brilliant red patch over each eye, which is retained throughout the year. The female's summer plumage is warmer, with brown and yellow speckling all over the body except for her white wings. In the winter, both sexes are snowy white, although the male has a black tail and retains the red eye patch. This makes it hard to distinguish them from the Willow Grouse. However, Ptarmigans are smaller with a thinner bill.

The bird can only be found at high altitudes and on desolate moors in the far north of Scotland.

Male

Female

DOTTEREL *Charadrius morinellus*

Unusually, in this species it is the female, not the male, which boasts the brighter colouring. She has a deep-orange chest fading into a charcoal belly, light buff upper, white throat and sharply defined face pattern with bold eye stripes. The male is darker and duller with less distinctive features, while the juvenile has a pale V-marking on the back of the head.

With its friendly nature and cheerful *witiwee* chatter, the Dotterel is a welcome but hard-to-spot visitor. It settles in small flocks on high mountains where it is unlikely to be seen by any but the most intrepid enthusiast. However, once located, the bird is remarkably tame, approaching humans within a couple of metres when beckoned by a simulated Dotterel call.

SNOW BUNTING *Plectrophenax nivalis*

From a dark-grey juvenile with stumpy body and legs, the male blossoms into a stunning bird whatever the season. In winter, it has a light tan back with russet markings, orangey or reddish brown head, yellow bill and snowy white wings with broad black-fingered wingtips. In summer, it is completely dressed in black and white – black upper and wing tips; white head, wings and underside. The female's winter plumage is darker than the male's. The head is brown and her back has black and brown streaks, which appear greyer in the summer.

In summer, the Snow Bunting is generally found in the highest regions of northern Scotland where snow may linger, but it migrates for the winter to sheltered marshes by the French coast, or to lowland areas of East Europe.

NIGHTJAR *Caprimulgus europaeus*

This graceful, medium-sized bird is hard to spot, as it is dormant during the day, only emerging at dusk to hunt around trees and bushes for moths to eat on the wing. Its mottled, barred and striped plumage resembles bark or leaves, providing the perfect camouflage against its typical heathland habitat. Both sexes have intricate, almost geometric, markings in brown and grey, with white beading on each side of the body, pale cheek marks, small downward pointed bill and a flat head. In flight, however, the male has clearly defined white marks on the wingtips along with white tail corners, features that are missing in the female. With their long tails and narrow wings, Nightjars are strikingly elegant.

From spring to autumn, it resides on open ground, heaths and forest clearings through most of Britain except for Scotland and the far north of England. The nightjar is a very nosy bird and after dusk will closely inspect any human visitors to its territory.

BIRDS OF PREY

BUZZARD *Buteo buteo*

Buzzards are instantly recognizable from their effortless flight: long, slow flaps of their wing make them look almost lazy. When quartering moorland, the buzzard will either be hovering above potential prey or using thermal air currents to soar in circles. When prey is sighted it can instantly fold its wings and stoop or dive to capture its prey, which can be as small as a beetle. After myxomatosis decimated the rabbit population in the 1950s, Buzzard numbers dwindled as the loss of its primary food source took its toll. However, modern methods of combating myxomatosis mean that numbers are increasing again.

Oddly for such a large and voracious predator, the Buzzard will usually fly off when mobbed by gulls or crows. If it cannot outfly them, however, it will turn and attack with its talons.

EGGS   Usually 2–3 eggs laid April to May

SONG   A plaintive, somewhat eerie *pieeou*

DIET   Small mammals, mainly rabbits; also sheep carrion, and occasionally birds, worms, caterpillars, lizards and beetles

HABITAT   Farmland, moorland and sometimes wooded hills in Wales, the Lake District, Scotland and South-West England

GOLDEN EAGLE *Aquila chrysaetos*

The Golden Eagle is without doubt the most majestic of all the native birds of prey. It is easily identified as it soars above the Scottish Highlands by the splayed primary feathers at the tip of its huge wings. When it has sighted its quarry it swoops at speeds of up to 144 kilometres per hour (90 miles per hour) and thumps down, pinning its prey to the ground.

Golden Eagles pair for life and usually have two or three eyries at heights of 1,500–2,000 feet which they use in rotation. The eyries can become quite large as the birds add to them each time they are used. The first chick is dominant, with the second usually only having a 20% chance of surviving its first few weeks.

EGGS   In March lays 2 eggs, 3–4 days apart

SONG   A staccato, high pitched *wieeou chip pip pip*

DIET   Blue hare, grouse, ptarmigan and other birds; small mammals and carrion; occasionally lambs, although usually only the weakest

HABITAT   Mountains and moorlands of the Scottish Highlands and islands, although some birds fly as far south as Cumbria

RED KITE *Milvus milvus*

During the Elizabethan period, Kites were a common sight scavenging in the streets of London. After centuries of decline, which saw them confined to Wales, a successful reintroduction scheme has seen numbers and range increase significantly.

Beautiful and graceful in flight, the Kite circles endlessly, searching for prey as it steers with its forked tail. On sighting prey, it swoops at speed and pounces on the prey. The apparent effortlessness of this flight pattern long ago gave the name to a popular children's toy: the kite.

EGGS   Lays 2–3 eggs in April or May

SONG   A whistling *pieeou* made in short bursts

DIET   Carrion, worms and small mammals

HABITAT   Uplands and hills in central Wales, central Scotland and central England – most prevalent in the Chilterns; good places to see them are above the M40 motorway in Oxfordshire and at the Galloway Kite Trail.

HEN HARRIER *Circus cyaneus*

The Hen Harrier gets its name from its habit of predating free-range fowl, although in modern times it has been persecuted for causing a decline in shooting stocks of grouse. Sexes are easily distinguished: males are pale grey, females and juveniles are brown with a white rump and long barred tail.

Courtship displays are spectacular with the birds climbing steeply in the air, turning and somersaulting at the top before plummeting with wings closed. In normal flight, the Hen Harrier makes four or five wing beats, gliding at low level with wings half-raised before pouncing on prey, or occasionally taking a bird from the air. While the female is on the nest, the male will call to her after making a kill and pass the prey to her mid-flight.

EGGS   Lays 4 eggs between May and June

SONG   Likened to *rrrreee chit chit chit rrree*

DIET   Mainly small ground-dwelling mammals and a few birds which are caught on the wing; occasionally eggs and the young of other birds

HABITAT   During the breeding season, upland moorland; otherwise lowland heath, farmland, coastal marshes and fenland

WETLAND BIRDS

Life thrives in wet places. Fish, small invertebrates, insects, frogs, crustaceans and molluscs all love the damp, and these creatures provide a valuable food source for larger creatures, including many birds. Spend time by a river, a lake, or even an old gravel pit, and you may see the flash of a Kingfisher as it dives for fish, hear the cooo-leee of the Curlew, or spot the slow flapping of wings as a Heron passes above you.

THE WETLAND HABITAT

Wetland is any area of land which is saturated, either permanently or seasonally – rivers, lakes, marshes, bog and fen – containing fresh, salt or brackish water. Wetlands provide British birds with a hugely significant habitat – indeed they contain the widest variety of wildlife outside our oceans – and are critically important to maintaining biodiversity. They provide shelter, food and breeding ground for many bird species.

Over the years, the area of wetland available to bird life has been drastically reduced to make way for human needs. Redevelopment through dredging, farming and construction has led to the loss of over half of all original wetland habitat. The UK has lost over a third of its ponds since the Second World War, and the traditional village pond has suffered especially. In addition, pesticides, herbicides and fertilizers from farmland all get washed into the surviving wetlands, causing pollution and destroying wildlife further.

Fragmentation of our wetlands has contributed to a decrease in populations of wading birds. Smaller areas mean that more birds nest closer to the fringes of the wetland, where eggs are more accessible to predators.

This destruction of habitat has a detrimental effect on human life also, as wetland offers protection against flooding, prevents soil erosion and soaks up contaminants that would otherwise find their way into our drinking water. As a result, real efforts are now being made to protect what is left of our wetlands.

How birds are adapting

The sheer biological richness of wetlands makes them some of the most popular sites for birdwatchers, with a greater variety of bird species to be seen here than in any other habitat. Most notably, wetlands provide resting and feeding areas for migratory birds, which may use this type of habitat as a temporary stopping place or spend many months here, breeding.

Many indigenous species, such as Grebes, exist only in wetlands and depend solely on this habitat for their continued survival. However, with the loss of natural wetlands, Grebes, as well as Divers, are adapting to human-made wetlands such as gravel pits. Even though most gravel pits are close to urban and agricultural environments, they are home to a wide variety of species, often at high breeding densities. These new human-made habitats will be vitally important for the

future conservation of marshland and aquatic species, and may act as reservoirs of diversity in the future. As a result, these man-made sites should be seen as just as important in conservation terms as natural wetland sites. The key to the future could be a mix of conservation and recreation, with the aim of developing more successful breeding grounds for our wetland birds.

Conservation initiatives

Not all birds can adapt to human-made wetlands, and ongoing initiatives aim to protect our existing natural wetlands. One initiative in Cambridgeshire is planning to join up two existing wetland reserves that were once part of the Great Fen of Cambridgeshire, a massive wetland area that was drained in the seventeenth century to make way for farming. If successful, this will create a new huge wetland and provide a vital and enhanced habitat for many rare and endangered species.

It is a long-term project involving the removal of a three-kilometre wide corridor of land from agricultural production and allowing it to flood in order to create a reed-covered wetland of 3,000 hectares. The project will significantly raise water levels, bringing back reeds, grasses and many rare plants.

One species that will benefit greatly from this project is the Bittern, a bird that came close to extinction in the 1990s. Many waders, such as Snipe and Lapwing, should also see their numbers increase. Although one main focus of the plan is conservation of wetland and wetland species, recreation and tourism will play a role too.

These are all welcome initiatives, but much more needs to be done. Simply providing new habitats and revitalising former ones is not enough. Degradation of habitat through water pollution, pesticides and heavy metals is destroying food sources and marine life, such as eels. Legislation needs to be introduced to limit the contaminants that enter ground water. However, there is some good news too: action already taken is working, with a 47% increase in the number of breeding Bitterns in the past ten years.

BARNACLE GOOSE   *Branta leucopsis*

ADULT   The Barnacle Goose is medium in size compared to other geese. The adult of both sexes has a white face and black head, neck and breast, with a pale grey or white underside. The back and wings are silver, with black bars across both. The tail is white and tipped with black, and there is a V-shaped black marking on the rump. The bill is black, with a small line of black leading from its base to the eye.

JUVENILE   Juveniles are similar, although their colourings are less even and appear duller.

EGGS   Barnacle Geese nest in small colonies on rocks, or high on cliffs ledges, away from predators such as the Arctic Fox. Nests are built by the female and usually lined with grass, moss or lichen. The female incubates the creamy-white eggs alone for between 21 and 28 days, but both parents feed the young.

SONG   The call of the Barnacle Goose is a gruff, barking *kaw*. When the call is made during flight (they fly in flocks, in dense irregular patterns, not in a V formation) it receives a quick response from others, on a large scale.

DIET   Barnacle Geese eat mainly leaves and stems of aquatic plants, as well as other grasses. In winter, they sometimes feed on grain and vegetables.

LENGTH	**58–71 cm (23–28 in)**
WINGSPAN	**138 cm (54 in)**
BREEDING STARTS	**May**
NUMBER OF EGGS PER CLUTCH	**4**

Where in UK Barnacle Geese can be seen	Months when Barnacle Geese can be seen

HABITAT   These geese are migratory visitors from northern areas such as Norway, Greenland and Russia, spending the winter in the warmer climate of Scotland, Ireland and the Netherlands. The best place to see Barnacle Geese is undoubtedly on the Solway Firth. They are also present in large numbers on the Isle of Islay in Scotland, and across the north-west coast of the Scottish mainland, where they can be seen feeding on land and in water, commonly on marsh ground.

OTHER   Because Barnacle Geese lay their eggs high up to avoid predation, young goslings must leap down to the ground to feed. The soft down and light weight of the goslings is often enough to allow them to float to the ground without harm, but sometimes they are not so lucky.

BRENT GOOSE *Branta bernicla*

ADULT The small Brent Goose is almost entirely black-brown in colour, aside from a thin white collar across the front half of the throat, a broad white underside and a thin white strip on the breast along the line of the wing. It may have either a pale or dark belly, and adults have a small white neck patch.

JUVENILE In juveniles, the wing has thin white bands along the width and there is no white neck patch.

EGGS Brent Geese nest on the ground, close to water, in a shallow depression lined with grass, moss and down. Both parents build the nest but only the female will incubate the eggs. These are usually a cream or yellow-white, but can also be a pale olive colour. After about 24 to 26 days the eggs hatch and both parents feed the young.

SONG The call is a rhythmic croaking.

DIET They eat aquatic plants such as algae and seaweed, as well as eel grass and mosses.

HABITAT Brent Geese are migratory, spending the winter in the UK before returning to their widespread breeding grounds. They are most commonly sighted on estuaries and salt marshes, in places such as the Wash on the east coast of England, and across various sites in south-eastern England. In the north and west, they can be found on Lindisfarne in Northumberland and in Northern Ireland.

OTHER In flight, the Brent Goose does not fly in a rigid V formation like some larger geese: rather, it forms large flocks which are irregularly distributed and sometimes very dense.

LENGTH	55–66 cm (22–26 in)
WINGSPAN	115 cm (45 in)
BREEDING STARTS	June
NUMBER OF EGGS PER CLUTCH	3–5

Where in UK Brent Geese can be seen

J
F
M
A
M
J
J
A
S
O
N
D

Months when Brent Geese can be seen

COOT *Fulica atra*

ADULT The Coot is a round, dumpy bird, mainly black or dark grey, with a striking white bill and facial shield. This gave rise to the expression 'bald as a coot' ('bald' is an old word for white), a saying that goes back to the fifteenth century. The wings are pale grey below, and the legs are grey and yellow. The iris in the eye is a distinctive red. The feet are large and broad, and without webbing, which is unusual for a water bird. Instead, a large lobe on the toes assists with swimming. Both sexes of adults are similar.

JUVENILE Juveniles are a dark grey rather than black, and have more white colouring on the face and breast.

EGGS Nests are built in shallow water, and constructed from plant matter. They are usually within the shelter of long aquatic plants and grasses, although sometimes they will be built in the open. The Coot's eggs are buff with brown spots. Both parents incubate the eggs and both feed the young. The newly-hatched offspring will be led to water by the male. Coots may lay two or three clutches in a season.

LENGTH	36–38 cm (14–15 in)
WINGSPAN	70–80 cm (28–31 in)
BREEDING STARTS	March
NUMBER OF EGGS PER CLUTCH	5–15

J F M A M J J A S O N D

Where in UK Coots can be seen

Months when Coots can be seen

SONG Coots have many varying calls, but the most common are a loud, metallic *pit* or a deep *kowk*. Juveniles often emit a high-pitched whistling sound.

DIET The diet is aquatic plants such as duckweed, grasses and aquatic invertebrates including snails and larvae brought up from the waterbed.

HABITAT The best place to spot a Coot is in long grass or other vegetation by the water's edge, usually a pond or reservoir. When startled, they will run quickly towards water.

OTHER Coots can become extremely territorial and aggressive during the breeding season, and there can be a lot of violent fighting between males. They have very large feet, which can cause them to look cumbersome when walking. Coots are closely related to the smaller Moorhen, which has a red facial shield where the Coot's is white. They share similar diets, but Coots rarely compete for food with Moorhens.

CURLEW   *Numenius arquata*

ADULT This large wader has an exceptionally long, narrow, sickle-shaped bill which curves downwards at the tip to help the bird forage through peat and mud. The female tends to have a slightly longer bill than the male but, apart from this, there is little to tell the sexes apart; both have the same streaky brown plumage, fading to a white rump that is clearly visible in flight.

JUVENILE In juveniles the sexes are similar, sporting the same long legs, the distinctive barred tail and pale mottled wings.

EGGS Curlews lay green and brown eggs in a shallow scrape in a meadow or similar place; the young leave their nest soon after hatching.

SONG The haunting *cooo-leee* is just part of the Curlew's repertoire. When courting, the male serenades his mate with trilling cries as he swoops from a tremendous height with outstretched wings.

DIET Using their long narrow beaks, Curlews probe through mud for worms and insects. They also eat small crabs if available.

HABITAT Curlews can be seen in the UK all year round, although they only remain in their breeding habitat in the spring months. In June, immediately after nesting, females head for the coast, leaving their mates behind to care for the fledglings. Although some Curlews overwinter in the UK, others migrate to warmer climes, such as the Mediterranean or West Africa, returning in February or later.

LENGTH	50–60 cm (20–24 in)
WINGSPAN	100 cm (39 in)
BREEDING STARTS	April
NUMBER OF EGGS PER CLUTCH	3–6

Where in UK
Curlew
can be seen

Months when
Curlew
can be seen

OTHER Outside the breeding season, Curlews are often seen in small flocks and will congregate with other waders. In these congregations, Curlews can be hard to distinguish from Whimbrels. But Curlews are bigger and have no stripes on the crown; their song is also distinctive. In flight, Curlews can reach very high altitudes, crossing mountains up to 600 m (20,000 ft) high.

GREAT CRESTED GREBE *Podiceps cristatus*

ADULT The Great Crested Grebe is an elegant aquatic bird with a very distinctive appearance: a crest is its most notable feature. Adults have long, slender necks which are white on the front and dark behind. In summer they have a black cap and a bright white face, with a copper patch lined with black. The bill is long and spiked, with a black strip extending from the base to the eye. In winter, the copper parts fade to white.

JUVENILE Juveniles are similar, although they have zebra-like black and white striped markings on the face and neck, paler grey upper parts and a paler crest. They also lack the strip around the eye.

EGGS Great Crested Grebes nest on water. They construct floating platforms from aquatic plants amongst dense vegetation. The birds cover their white eggs in rotting vegetation to keep them warm, and both parents will incubate them when required, seldom leaving the nest other than to gather food. Very young Grebes can be seen riding on their parents' backs.

SONG The Grebe makes a loud rattle, almost like a *kaw*, which ends with a single rapid sound.

DIET The main item of diet is fish, but Grebes will also eat small invertebrates, insects and frogs.

HABITAT Great Crested Grebes are a common sight around water across England and Wales, but less so in Scotland or Ireland. They can be seen mainly on rivers, ponds and lakes, in both rural and urban areas.

OTHER The legs of the Great Crested Grebe are placed quite far back on their bodies, which makes them awkward on land. When they feel threatened, they will head for water rather than flying away, often diving underwater and resurfacing a good distance from where they entered the water. Grebes were once hunted for their feathers, which were used as decoration in hats. They were almost wiped out in the UK, but conservation methods allowed the population to recover.

LENGTH	46–61 cm (18–24 in)
WINGSPAN	59–73 cm (23–29 in)
BREEDING STARTS	April
NUMBER OF EGGS PER CLUTCH	4

J
F
M
A
M
J
J
A
S
O
N
D

Where in UK
Great Crested Grebes
can be seen

Months when
Great Crested Grebe
can be seen

GREY HERON *Ardea cinerea*

ADULT The Grey Heron is the largest heron in Europe. Male and female adults look the same: predominantly pale grey but with a long and slender white neck showing black markings on the front. The yellow bill is sharp and dagger-like, and this becomes brighter in spring. The head is white, with a black supercilium across the eye, leading to a crest. The wings are darker below, and around the edges, with a small white patch on the leading edge. The feet are large and broad.

JUVENILE In juveniles the grey plumage is darker and extends along the neck. The bill is also darker, and there is no crest.

EGGS Pale green-blue eggs are laid on platform nests which both parents have built from twigs and grass in a tall tree. Both parents incubate the eggs and feed the young.

SONG The call is usually heard when the Heron is in flight; it is best described as a loud, harsh *fraank*.

LENGTH	90–95 cm (35–37 in)
WINGSPAN	175–195 cm (69–77 in)
BREEDING STARTS	February
NUMBER OF EGGS PER CLUTCH	2–7

J
F
M
A
M
J
J
A
S
O
N
D

Where in UK
Grey Heron
can be seen

Months when
Grey Heron
can be seen

DIET The diet is mostly fish, frogs and other aquatic creatures (Herons are notorious for plundering garden ponds for fish). They will also hunt small mammals and sometimes other birds.

HABITAT Grey Herons prefer river margins, lakes and marshes but can also be found by the coast and on estuaries. During the breeding season you may spot several huddling together in a 'heronry'. In flight they are very noticeable as they are so big and move with slow, deeply arched wings; the flight is more leisurely than that of most large raptors. They fly with the head drawn back so that the neck forms an S shape, with the feet trailing behind.

OTHER When hunting, Grey Herons remain completely motionless as they wait for the perfect moment to strike. If they choose to stalk their prey, they wade slowly through the water.

KINGFISHER *Alcedo atthis*

ADULT Kingfishers are easily recognized by their striking plumage and distinctive shape. Adult Kingfishers have a striking electric blue across the back, rump, wings and head, with a brighter strip along the centre of the back. They have a bright orange breast and underside, and the wings also have this orange plumage beneath. The bill is long and pointed: the male's being black and the female's a more reddish colour. The face is orange, with a white band below. The blue colouring from the back extends through this white band to the base of the bill. Their heads are disproportionately large in relation to their bodies, and their tails are short.

JUVENILE In juveniles the plumage is less vibrant.

EGGS Kingfishers nest in burrows dug into banks, as much as a metre (40 inches) long. These burrows are made by both parents and are not lined. This soon changes however, as undigested fish bones are regurgitated and accumulate in the nest. The eggs are smooth and white, and both parents incubate them, then later feed the young.

SONG The call is a sharp, high-pitched *chik-eeee*. If you are walking on a river bank, this may well be the first indicator of a Kingfisher's presence.

LENGTH	16–17 cm (6 –7 in)
WINGSPAN	24–26 cm (9–10 in)
BREEDING STARTS	April
NUMBER OF EGGS PER CLUTCH	6–7

J
F
M
A
M
J
J
A
S
O
N
D

Where in UK
Kingfishers
can be seen

Months when
Kingfishers
can be seen

DIET The diet is freshwater fish but Kingfishers will also eat aquatic insects and, on rare occasions, crustaceans, molluscs and small amphibians.

HABITAT Kingfishers like slow-moving rivers, where they perch on branches hanging over or near the water, watching and waiting for prey. They may also be seen flying low along the surface of the water. Kingfishers can also be found around still bodies of water, such as gravel pits, ponds and lakes.

OTHER Kingfishers are most often seen as a flash of colour as they dive into the water with great speed after a fish. When a fish is caught, the Kingfisher will return to the perch, then stun the prey, before swallowing it headfirst. This is all possible because of their specially-adapted vision, which allows them to see their underwater prey clearly.

LAPWING *Vanellus vanellus*

ADULT Also known as the Peewit or the Green Plover, the Lapwing is a very distinctive bird of farmland and marshes. The adult male has a white face which is framed with black, with iridescent green and purple plumage on the back and wings. This appears black from a distance. The throat is also black, with a white breast and underside. There is a noticeable orange-brown colour beneath the tail. Adult females are similar, but with duller faces. Both adults display long crests, which are the most recognizable feature of the Lapwing.

JUVENILE Juveniles are similar to adults, although the face is more buff than white, and the crest is not yet fully developed.

EGGS Lapwings will nest anywhere that is open, bare and damp, from meadows and marshes to industrial sites. Both parents help to build the nest, which is made in a shallow hole in the ground, and then both incubate the eggs, which are stone-coloured with black blotches. Both also share in the feeding of the young.

SONG The song is a loud, raucous *pee-wit*, which gives it one of its names. The call is a sharp, nasal *peet*.

DIET Lapwings feed on a variety of invertebrates found either on or close to the ground surface, including earthworms, caterpillars, beetles and flies.

LENGTH	28–31 cm (11–12 in)
WINGSPAN	70–76 cm (28–30 in)
BREEDING STARTS	March
NUMBER OF EGGS PER CLUTCH	2–5

Where in UK Lapwings can be seen

Months when Lapwings can be seen

HABITAT The best place to spot a Lapwing is on open ground, often near a water source. They also gather in huge numbers on marshland.

OTHER Lapwings are very protective of their nests. If nesting in meadows on or near farmland, Lapwings will defend their nests against large animals including horses or cattle, usually successfully. If a predator shows interest in the nest, Lapwings will employ a clever strategy of feigning injury, moving away from the nest in a manner which suggests it is injured, usually by trailing a wing as if broken. When the predator has been led far from the nest, the Lapwing will fly away.

MALLARD   *Anas platyrhynchos*

ADULT   The Mallard is one of the best-known wetland birds in Britain. The male is easily recognizable with its glossy green head and thin white collar. Below this is a brown breast and a grey underside. The wings and back are grey, with a blue-purple patch across them, lined on both sides in white. A broad, dark strip runs down the centre of the back to a dark tail. The female shares the male's wing markings, but is a mottled buff colour, with dark brown streaks on the throat, breast, wings and tail. The male's bill is yellow, whereas the female's is brown, and the legs of both are orange.

JUVENILE   Juveniles are similar in appearance to the female, but lack the markings on the wings.

EGGS   Nests are made in a variety of places, from open ground to dense vegetation, and even in trees. They are constructed from twigs and grass, and lined with down. The female builds this nest and in it lays her light grey-green, white or pale blue eggs. She then incubates these eggs alone. The ducklings are independent as soon as they are hatched but the mother will remain fiercely protective of them until they are grown.

SONG   The female gives a loud, coarse quack, while the male whistles.

DIET   Mallards eat a wide variety of food such as acorns, berries and seeds. They also eat shellfish and aquatic plants and even frogs.

LENGTH	50–65 cm (20–26 in)
WINGSPAN	81–98 cm (32–38 in)
BREEDING STARTS	February
NUMBER OF EGGS PER CLUTCH	9–13

J
F
M
A
M
J
J
A
S
O
N
D

Where in UK
Mallard
can be seen

Months when
Mallard
can be seen

HABITAT   It is easy to spot a Mallard – they can be found on or around water almost everywhere, including urban locations. They are highly adaptable birds, and tolerate humans well, which partly accounts for their large numbers.

OTHER   Mallards can often be seen searching for food underwater. They submerge headfirst, leaving their rump pointing upwards, as they look for plants, shellfish or frogs. They are highly gregarious and gather in large numbers: a group of Mallards is known as a 'sord'.

MOORHEN *Gallinula chloropus*

ADULT The Moorhen is a small waterfowl with a short neck and small head. It has longish greeny-yellow legs with long, narrow toes and no webbing. The adult male is a greeny-brown colour with a bright red bill and facial shield. The wings have a white stripe and the undertail is white. The female also has the distinctive red bill but is a paler greeny-brown with a cream wing stripe and undertail. The Moorhen looks superficially like the Common Coot, which is a larger and more aggressive bird of similar shape. However, both male and female Coots are dark grey or black with a white frontal shield.

JUVENILE Juveniles are pale grey-brown – similar to the adult female, but with a darker head.

EGGS Moorhens lay their large clutch of eggs in a nest of twigs and grass, hidden within rushes or waterside vegetation. The eggs themselves are pale yellow with rusty brown and black spots. The young when they hatch are black and fluffy, with red bills and blue eye patches, and are soon very active and mobile.

SONG The Moorhen is quite bold and noisy, and often shrieks a sharp *ik ik ik*, maintaining audible contact with other Moorhens when these are out of sight amongst the waterside greenery. When annoyed it can stretch out its call to a long *kyaaar*.

LENGTH	28–35 cm (11–14 in)
WINGSPAN	48–55 cm (19–22 in)
BREEDING STARTS	March
NUMBER OF EGGS PER CLUTCH	7–12

J
F
M
A
M
J
J
A
S
O
N
D

Where in UK Moorhens can be seen

Months when Moorhens can be seen

DIET The diet is various water plants supplemented by insects and invertebrates.

HABITAT The Moorhen is found on all wetlands and waterways in the UK.

OTHER As with other members of the family of Rails, this bird likes to pick over marshy ground and grassy areas near water, walking very deliberately, and spreading its weight carefully as though it might sink. On every step it bobs its head and flicks its short tail, which it holds cocked up high. Moorhens are quite happy walking on floating vegetation, but can also swim well. Flying seems to take more effort and take-off can involve a long run-up, often across water. When alarmed, Moorhens dive underwater and move off before re-appearing a short distance away.

WATER RAIL *Rallus aquaticus*

ADULT The Water Rail is a squat little bird with a short tail, stubby wings and a long neck. It is coloured a rusty brown with dark brown scalloping, slate grey breast and underside, barred flanks and a creamy-white or yellow undertail. The long red bill has a dark tip and is curved slightly downwards. Colouration of the female is similar to the male, but she is a little duller and usually smaller in size.

JUVENILE Juveniles are paler brown and their barring is a little more extensive on the grey-brown chest. They have a plain buff bill.

EGGS The nest is made of stalks and grass, hidden within reeds or waterside vegetation. The eggs are pale yellow with blue, brown and black speckles.

SONG Water Rails are frequently heard before they are seen, emitting a characteristic squeal from their hiding place in waterside foliage. They also make a variety of other noises resembling other water fowl: short *ip ip ip* sounds and longer fading trills.

DIET They live on a diet of shoots, seeds and berries, supplemented with insects and invertebrates and occasional small animals.

HABITAT Water Rails frequent fresh and saltwater marshes and wetlands. Although they hide in reeds, rushes and waterside vegetation, they will venture out on forays for food. Their narrow shape allows them to slip easily through dense stands of reeds and rushes.

OTHER When walking, these birds flick their short cocked tails and bob their heads either slowly and deliberately, or speedily as they dash for cover. Their flight is direct, with rapid wingbeats with legs dangling behind.

LENGTH	24–28 cm (9–11 in)
WINGSPAN	40–43 cm (16–17 in)
BREEDING STARTS	March
NUMBER OF EGGS PER CLUTCH	6–12

J
F
M
A
M
J
J
A
S
O
N
D

Where in UK
Water Rails
can be seen

Months when
Water Rails
can be seen

SHELDUCK *Tadorna tadorna*

ADULT Shelducks are large, brightly coloured ducks. The adults are piebald, showing white bodies with a bold chestnut-brown breast band, two thick black bands on the back and a black outside to their pointy white wings. The heads and long necks are greeny-black with bright red bills; the legs and webbed feet are pink. The male has a bright red bill knob on top of his bill; in the female this knob is smaller. The Shelduck is not often confused with other ducks, due to its size, but can look similar to Shoveler ducks at a glance, which have similar colouration.

JUVENILE The juvenile has less distinct markings, with a creamy bill, and brown scalloped feathers on the upper body. They are generally duller and have more extensive white plumage stretching up under the neck and face.

EGGS Shelducks generally build nests of dried grass and duck down in hollows or old rabbit burrows, among sand dunes or on grassy banks. The eggs are large and creamy coloured. The chicks, when mobile, are often kept in crèches of large numbers while parents take turns to guard.

SONG Shelducks are gregarious and noisy, often quacking *ak ak ak ak* and hissing at each other. They also have an array of more personal whistles.

DIET They particularly favour small marine molluscs, but also eat insects, crustaceans, fish and worms and freshwater vegetation. They filter feed in shallow water, disturbing the sediment as they go.

LENGTH	56–68 cm (22–27 in)
WINGSPAN	100–125 cm (39–49 in)
BREEDING STARTS	May
NUMBER OF EGGS PER CLUTCH	8–15

J F M A M J J A S O N D

Where in UK Shelducks can be seen

Months when Shelducks can be seen

HABITAT Shelducks are commonly seen in mixed groups, feeding in shallow water on coastal wetlands, estuaries and intertidal coastal zones. They can also be seen grazing fields and marshy shores in the same manner as geese.

OTHER In the air, Shelducks move with slow wingbeats, flying in formation over distances. They do migrate, but not very far, most flocking in tidal estuaries for moulting.

REDSHANK *Tringa totanus*

ADULT The Redshank is a medium-sized wading bird that, true to its name, stands on long, bright red legs. It is speckled brown, darker on top, speckled white underneath, and the black eye has a white rim and faint fore-stripe. The bill is long and red with a black tip. In flight the Redshank shows dark speckled brown, a white oval on its rump and tapered wings with white trailing panels that are completely white underneath.

JUVENILE The juvenile is a more speckly brown colour than the adult, with a dark bill and slightly duller orange legs.

EGGS The eggs are small and conical, coloured a glossy buff and covered with varied brown splotches. They are laid in a hollow nest of dried grass well concealed in damp vegetation. The adults guard the area with zeal, calling hysterically and drawing the attention of intruders away from the nest or young.

SONG Redshanks are renowned for their persistent alarm, piping *pyu pyuu pyuuu* as soon as any intruder is sighted. They also communicate with each other with various trills and twitters.

DIET The diet consists of invertebrates, small fish and amphibians plus seeds, berries and a little tender vegetation.

LENGTH	24–27 cm (9–101 in)
WINGSPAN	47–53 cm (19–21 in)
BREEDING STARTS	April
NUMBER OF EGGS PER CLUTCH	3–4

J
F
M
A
M
J
J
A
S
O
N
D

Where in UK Redshanks can be seen

Months when Redshanks can be seen

HABITAT Redshanks are found on most coasts, estuaries and wetlands. They often gather in mixed flocks of waders, chasing the waves up and down in the intertidal zone on beaches.

OTHER They are very active birds with a constant nervous head and tail bobbing, even in flight. This flight involves short, rapid, shallow wingbeats with stiff wings swept slightly back, and the bird usually calls as it flies. When it lands it often leaves both wings held high for a moment before carefully folding them over its back.

MUTE SWAN *Cygnus olor*

ADULT Mute swans are the largest of the swans and easily distinguished by their large, black-outlined, orange bill and long, serpentine neck. The male has a large black knob on top of the bill.

JUVENILE Juveniles are coloured a dull brown with a beige bill. They gradually gain white adult plumage over several years.

EGGS The nest is an elaborate affair by the water's edge, built on a huge platform of twigs and branches, which lifts it up above the water. This nest is lined with grass and downy feathers, and in it are laid large oval, pale grey eggs, often slightly dirty looking.

SONG Mute swans are misnamed as they are far from quiet. They make various sounds, including a bark, a hink and a trumpeting; they will hiss loudly when feeling threatened.

DIET The principle diet is grasses and aquatic plants. They will dabble for food, or upend, using their long neck to reach deeper vegetation.

HABITAT Swans are found on rivers and lakes throughout the UK.

OTHER These birds can be very territorial and will display, with raised wings, and head and neck drawn back, whilst advancing strongly towards the intruder. This is often accompanied by hissing and rustling of wing feathers. They are strong swimmers, thanks to their large black webbed feet. But getting airborne can be quite a feat and Swans will often opt for a long run over the water to gain enough speed to get airborne. Conversely, when landing, they come in on a long glide, water-skiing to a stop on their webbed feet. When in the air, they thrust their heads and necks straight forward, legs tucked back, and fly with long powerful wingbeats, often producing a thrumming noise. They often fly in formation, and will migrate long distances, mostly to favoured moulting areas.

LENGTH	140–160 cm (55–63 in)
WINGSPAN	200–240 cm (79–94 in)
BREEDING STARTS	April
NUMBER OF EGGS PER CLUTCH	5–11

Where in UK
Mute Swans
can be seen

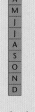

Months when
Mute Swans
can be seen

TEAL   *Anas crecca*

ADULT   The Teal is the country's smallest duck. The breeding plumage of the drake is very striking: a chestnut head with a dark green mask, outlined in gold, extending down the back of the neck. The feathers of the breast and wings look grey, but really they are very finely striped black and white. Smart black and white wing braces show when the wings are folded, the plumage of the breast is a spotty buff colour, and the undertail is striped yellow and black. The female has feathers that are brown with gold scalloping, but otherwise has wing markings similar to the male. Both have grey-black bills, short grey-black legs, and show white mid-wing bars and dark green and black wing panels on their upper wings. The underwings are pale grey with a white centre.

JUVENILE   Juveniles look very similar to a dull female.

EGGS   Teals nest by the water's edge. The neat little nests are made from grasses and grey down, and are extremely well concealed in grasses and reeds. The eggs are plain and creamy.

SONG   The sound is a reedy whistle and a bell-like *krik krik*. Teals also quack quietly amongst pairs and when in small groups – particularly the females.

DIET   These are dabbling ducks, stirring up sediment for seeds and aquatic vegetation, supplemented with insects and crustaceans.

HABITAT   Flocks of Teal can be found in fresh and brackish water in wetlands, estuaries and marshlands, rivers, lakes and ponds throughout the UK. They may move to higher marshy ground in summer.

OTHER   Teal tend to be nervous and will rise, almost vertically, into the air at the slightest disturbance. They tend to fly fast and direct with rapid wingbeats. Teal can migrate huge distances in flying formations, moving north east in the summer and returning in the winter, but many prefer to stay in the UK.

LENGTH	34–38 cm (13–15 in)
WINGSPAN	53–58 cm (21–23 in)
BREEDING STARTS	April
NUMBER OF EGGS PER CLUTCH	8–10

Where in UK Teal can be seen

Months when Teal can be seen

LESS COMMON BIRDS

AVOCET *Recurvirostra avosetta*

The Avocet is the most elegant of waders. Standing tall on long, fine, grey legs, both male and female birds are coloured a brilliant white with bold black stripes over the shoulders and wings. They have a black cap that extends down the back of the neck and a long fine bill that is markedly turned up at the tip.

Avocets feed by sweeping the tip of their bill from side to side as they walk through shallow water and mud, sifting for small crustaceans and invertebrates. Avocets migrate south for the winter, but can be found in selected wetlands around throughout the country.

LITTLE EGRET *Egretta garzetta*

Once plentiful, The Little Egret was hunted almost to extinction during the fashion craze for plumes on hats in the late Victorian and Edwardian eras. It is re-establishing itself well, and is now commonly found fishing on the coast, rivers and shorelines in the warmer south. It is a finely-built, heron-shaped bird with a long serpentine neck, long black bill and long black legs with oddly yellow feet. Both sexes look alike and have a couple of long white plumes hanging from the nape of the neck.

The Little Egret can be confused with its larger cousin, the Great White Egret, which has a longer neck and no plume. Also the Cattle Egret is now starting to appear in the UK; this looks similar to the Little Egret, but is bulkier, with a pale yellow or reddish bill and yellow legs.

RINGED PLOVER *Charadrius hiaticula*

Both sexes of Ringed Plover are grey on top and white below, with a thick black breast band and another band round the eyes. They have a short orange bill with a black tip and long orange legs. Their tapered wings are angled back in flight and show a white wing bar. The Little Ringed Plover is similar to the Ringed Plover, but smaller and less common.

Ringed Plovers are comical little birds that are frequently seen in small or mixed flocks running around the waterline on seashores and mudflats picking at the silt for small crustaceans, insects and worms. They move quickly, stopping periodically for a moment to look and listen, or tap the ground in front to disturb anything small and edible. In flight, they also move quickly, with sharp changes in direction.

PINTAIL *Anas acuta*

The Pintail is the size of a Mallard but with far greater poise and style. The adult male has a chocolate brown head with a white stripe starting at the back of the head and curving down the neck to widen out to join the white breast and grey flanks, which are in fact feathers that are very finely black and white striped. The feathers on the back are black with a white outline and a hint of yellow; there is an extended black, double tail spike.

The female Pintail is a bright scalloped brown all over, similar to female Mallards and Wigeon, but neater and longer in the neck.

Pintails are found on wetlands and waterways, migrating north in the summer to breed.

LITTLE GREBE *Tachybaptus ruficollis*

Little Grebes are commonly seen on wetlands and waterways all over the UK. They are very small, plump birds with a big head on a fairly longish neck and a very short tail. Both sexes are coloured dark brown above with pale underparts. The adult male has chestnut neck and cheeks and a very dark, almost black head. Both have a white spot next to the base of the bill.

Little Grebes are the smallest or the family of grebes; they have a busy nature and frequently squeal and trill at each other when in groups. The feed on small fish and crustaceans by diving for long periods and popping back up. They are very buoyant, with a very fluffy and blunt rear end, and are easily mistaken for ducklings.

POCHARD *Aythya ferina*

Pochards are small, dumpy diving ducks, very similar in shape and habit to the Tufted Duck. However, the plumage of the adult male is quite different to that of the Tufted Duck, showing a chestnut head and neck with a red eye. The breast and upper back, rump and tail is black and the rest of the body a delicately mottled grey. The female is a dun brown with pale underside, dark grey bill and black eye; she is easily confused with the Tufted Duck, although the latter is darker and has yellow eyes.

Pochards are common on wetlands and coastal marshes, often in mixed flocks with other ducks. They are quiet, occasionally making rattling sounds amongst each other. They dive or dabble for their food, which consists of small water insects, crustaceans and worms.

BIRDS OF PREY

MARSH HARRIER *Circus aeruginosus*

The Marsh Harrier is the largest of the harriers and can be recognized by its light flight with wings held in a V shape. It can be differentiated from other harriers by its heavier build and absence of white feathers on the rump. Females are larger than males and have creamier-looking head feathers.

The Marsh Harrier will quarter hunting grounds at low level, looking for the slightest ripple in the water that will give away a water vole.

In the 1800s, the draining of the Fens meant a huge decline in numbers. However, after a brief return in the 1920s, followed by a decline owing to pesticide use in the 1950s, the population is now at its most stable.

EGGS Four to five eggs laid between late April and June; young are fed by their mother until leaving the nest at 35–40 days

SONG A shrill *kwee-a*

DIET Small mammals, especially water voles; also Moorhens, Coots and other birds; also eggs, frogs, grass snakes

HABITAT Reed beds, marshland, wetland and farmland near to wetlands, mainly in eastern and south-eastern parts of the region, though some may be found in the north-west, south-west and in Scotland

SHORT-EARED OWL *Asio flammeus*

Commonly seen hunting in daylight, the Short-eared Owl is of medium size with a mottled brown body, pale under the wings, and yellow eyes.

When hunting, it circles, hovers and glides around its territory until prey is spotted. It will then twist its wings under its body so the wing-tips meet behind the tail, clapping them rapidly as it plunges like a stone.

The 'ears' which give this owl its name are merely small tufts of feathers with no aural function.

EGGS Four to eight eggs laid in a nest is a depression in the ground lined with vegetation

SONG Low, almost booming *hoo-hoo-hoo-hoo-hoo-hoo-hoo-ho*

DIET Mainly field voles; also other small mammals, birds and occasional insects

HABITAT In the breeding season, can be found in northern parts of the UK and on open moorland, grazing meadows and arable fields. The best chance of a sighting is in winter when these owls inhabit coastal marshes and wetland

OSPREY *Pandion haliaetus*

Ospreys are identifiable in flight by their long wings, which bend at the 'wrist', where there is a black patch of feathers which contrast with the white wing linings. At a distance they are sometimes mistaken for a large gull.

They are at their most spectacular when taking quarry. They fly and glide high above water to locate their prey, then half fold their wings and plunge almost vertically into the water with feet outstretched. The bird penetrates the water and grabs its prey, which it holds head first to carry to a perch or the eyrie. The Osprey has short spines on the underside of its toes which assist the long talons with grip and prevent the loss of a slippery prey. It can close its nostrils to prevent water getting in during a dive.

EGGS   The Osprey breeds by freshwater lochs and lakes, and sometimes on coastal brackish waters, laying 2 or 3 eggs in a nest known as an eyrie

SONG   An almost melodic *kee-koo-koo-koo-kooooo...kweee-kweee-kweee*

DIET   Medium-sized marine and freshwater fish

HABITAT   Freshwater, brackish and marine environments; best chances of a sighting are in Scotland, Cumbria and Rutland Water

MONTAGU'S HARRIER *Circus pygargus*

Named after the Devon naturalist, Colonel George Montagu, this is the smallest of the three UK harriers. A summer visitor, Montagu's Harrier is an extremely rare breeding bird in the UK with only 14 to 17 breeding pairs.

In flight it shows black wing tips and is distinguished from the hen harrier by its more pointed wings. In courtship displays, the male produces spectacular dives, loops and somersaults.

EGGS   Nests in open country, laying 4–5 eggs between late May and early June

SONG   A shrill *yick-yick-yick*

DIET   Small mammals, birds, frogs, some insects and worms

HABITAT   Southern and eastern UK, although nest areas are kept secret and are protected

SEA AND SHORE BIRDS

Seaside holidays in the UK are inevitably associated with the cry of seabirds. Even inland we may see gulls following behind a plough and picking up the small creatures turned up, or searching through rubbish in a tip. But how many of us can tell a Black-headed Gull from a Herring Gull or even from a Tern? In the next pages you can learn their similarities and differences, and much more besides.

THE SEA AND SHORE HABITAT

To bird lovers, the UK is fortunate to have a huge shoreline with varying habitats that suit a huge range of bird species. Cliffs, estuaries, salt marshes, rocky shores, sand dunes – all provide ideal homes for particular species.

Over 4,000 km of the coastline consists of cliffs, which form some of the most successful bird habitats, partly because the impact of humans has been minimal. Our cliffs teem with birds such as Gannets, Razorbills, Kittiwakes, Guillemots and Puffins. Good examples of these habitats are Bempton Cliffs in Yorkshire, Fowlsheugh in north-east Scotland and Dunnet Head, also in the north of Scotland. During the spring and summer months these areas become alive with many different species competing for space and food.

Cliffs suit birds which eat fish. Estuaries and salt marshes offer abundant food of a different nature, such as marine worms and tiny molluscs, which suit the waders and wildfowl that feed here in huge numbers from autumn to spring. In recent years, record numbers of specific species have been spotted in areas such as the Thames estuary, as

legislation introduced to clean up our rivers has improved the numbers of organisms on which the worms and molluscs feed – which in turn provide food for birds.

The position is not so good on our sea-shores where, although there is an abundance of food during intertidal times, bird numbers have been severely affected by human disturbance, both in the form of seaside redevelopment and recreation activities, especially during the summer months.

Life in coastal habitats

It is on cliffs and rocky islands where bird life has done best. Food is abundant, and breeding in large numbers helps to reduce the effects of predation – although humans, mammals and other birds do all predate the eggs of these birds.

Different species have adapted to particular niches on the coast. For example, Guillemots favour rocky ledges for their nests, while Puffins and Razorbills prefer grassy slopes where they can dig nesting burrows or re-use existing ones. Gulls form large, dense colonies to make the most of the available nesting space.

In estuaries, Dunlins feed at low tide, probing the muddy soil for worms, snails, molluscs and crustaceans, and

rest at high tide. Other birds, such as Sandpipers, tend to stay at the water's edge. Curlews have evolved longer beaks to probe deeper mud and get to less accessible food sources. These birds have all adapted in different ways in order to maximize the opportunities available.

Changing habitats

Over the last century and a half, much of the shoreline has been claimed for holiday developments, with the result that birds that depend on rock pools, sand dunes, rocky shores and beaches have suffered. Development has led to an increase in predators, such as cats and rats, as well as disturbance from humans, especially during the summer months. Plovers and Terns are two birds that are finding it increasingly difficult to establish successful nesting sites among sand dunes throughout the UK.

The cliffs have not been immune, with ribbon development, camp sites and holiday villages all appearing on cliff tops as well as by sandy beaches.

Estuaries and their inhabitants have suffered in a different way. Although a lot has been done to alleviate pollution from chemicals and sewage, more remains to be done. The continued siting of factories near estuaries is affecting bird numbers, as food sources become damaged. One species that has been affected severely is the Oystercatcher. However, this bird is fighting back by adapting to life inland.

Habitat fragmentation is another factor of modern life that affects shoreline species. With increasing densities of birds competing for food over smaller areas, aggression between species has led to less successful feeding and breeding.

In the past, we have taken our coastal ecosystems for granted – building houses and industries in flood-prone areas, damming and diverting rivers, and allowing polluted run-off from farming to spoil water quality. Now we are becoming aware that shorelines are sensitive areas with tremendous value for bird life, and that they need special care. Over recent years, legislation on pollution has improved the water quality of rivers, seas and estuaries, preventing the further decline of numerous species. Yet still further work remains to be done.

BLACK-HEADED GULL   *Croicocephalus ridibundus*

ADULT   The Black-headed Gull is relatively small, but extremely abundant. Both sexes have a black or dark brown hood in summer which fades throughout the season; in winter the Gull just has a black ear spot behind the eye, about the same size as the eye, which is also black. The wings have black tips to the primary feathers and a distinctive white leading edge, easily visible in flight. It also has a dark red beak and red legs which often show paler and even yellowish on birds out of season. This gull can be confused with the Mediterranean Gull, which is very similar but less common, and with the Little Gull; both these show black heads in summer but have paler wings with no white leading edge. Little Gulls are also much smaller and stockier.

JUVENILE   The juvenile Black-headed Gull has extensive speckled brown markings over wings, back and head, and a black tail band that is not present on the adult.

EGGS   Eggs are tapered ovoid and usually light greeny-brown with brown and grey spots. They are laid in a crude nest of grass set on the ground or set in reed beds.

SONG   The Black-headed Gull is very active, noisy and inquisitive, constantly laughing and cackling at other gulls – calls are a short *kak* and longer and much louder *kaar*.

DIET   These Gulls are successful foragers and scavengers, seeking out any easy pickings. They eat fish, worms, insects, seaweed, grass and refuse.

LENGTH	35–39 cm (14–15½ in)
WINGSPAN	86–99 cm (34–39 in)
BREEDING STARTS	April
NUMBER OF EGGS PER CLUTCH	3

J
F
M
A
M
J
J
A
S
O
N
D

Where in UK Black-headed Gulls can be seen

Months when Black-headed Gu can be seen

HABITAT   The Black–headed Gull is seen just about everywhere: on sewage works and waste tips, farms, wetlands and reservoirs, over cities as well as on all inland waterways and coastlines. They are very sociable and often flock in large numbers, frequently following tractors across newly ploughed fields or fishing boats out at sea or in harbour.

OTHER   The birds are agile flyers, and can often be seen soaring and circling high up or chasing each other for food. They are buoyant swimmers and like to stir up sediments with their feet in shallow water in the search for food.

COMMON GULL *Larus canus*

ADULT The Common Gull is a medium-sized, clean-featured seabird showing the classic pale 'seagull' grey upper body and wings. The mature adult of either sex has a white tail and underparts, slender wings with black tips showing a white spot or 'mirror', and a plain greeny-yellow bill and legs and a small black eye.

JUVENILE The juvenile gull shows extensive lines of grey-brown markings over the wings and head, a black tip to a dull or greyish bill, and a black tail band that is not present on the adult. Juveniles and adults off-season are easy to confuse with the Herring Gull, but the Herring Gull is larger, with a heavier aggressive-looking beak and general demeanour.

EGGS Common Gulls lay tapered ovoid eggs in pale colours varying from grey, brown-green to blue, with dark-brown spots and streaks. The nest is lined with grass and made in a small hollow or elevated on ledges and posts. Nesting colonies are small on rocky islands and moorland by preference.

SONG The Common Gull has a high-pitched *ke ke ke-aa* call and also a noisy squeal and mewling, particularly heard from immature or courting birds.

DIET Common Gulls are not fussy eaters and will eat fish, worms, insects, seeds and berries, grass and beach refuse and will also rob nests of other birds. Like other gulls, they scavenge and forage, and will chase other seabirds with food to get them to drop it. They don't often actively fish for live food.

LENGTH	40–46 cm (16–18 in)
WINGSPAN	99–108 cm (39–42½ in)
BREEDING STARTS	April
NUMBER OF EGGS PER CLUTCH	3

| J |
| F |
| M |
| A |
| M |
| J |
| J |
| A |
| S |
| O |
| N |
| D |

Where in UK Common Gulls can be seen

Months when Common Gulls can be seen

HABITAT Despite its name the Common Gull is not the most common gull, but it is widespread throughout the UK. They are usually spotted along coastlines, beaches and harbours, but are often found on sewage and waste tips, farms and wetlands, over cities as well as on inland waterways.

OTHER Common Gulls often flock in mixed groups of gulls, but not usually in large numbers. Couples call, posture and beg for food when courting, in a similar fashion to the Herring Gull.

GREAT BLACK-BACKED GULL *Larus marinus*

ADULT The Great Black-backed Gull is the largest seagull and is distinguishable from the Lesser Black-backed Gull by its slightly larger size. Another difference is leg colour: Great Black-backed Gulls have pink legs, while the Lesser have yellow legs. Both are equipped with a heavy, slightly hooked bill which is bright yellow with a strong red spot on the lower mandible. These birds are brilliant white, except for dark grey, almost black upper wings with large white spots or 'mirrors' on the tips. The black upper wings also show a white margin and the tail (on the adult) is completely white.

JUVENILE Juvenile Black-backed Gulls show a speckled brown tail and back, with a black tail band and lightly speckled underparts; they are similar to the Herring Gull, but with a whiter head. They take several years to reach full adult colouration, developing gradually increasing contrast.

EGGS The nests are generally on rocky prominences or cliffs and may be in mixed colonies with other seabirds. The large tapered ovoid eggs are usually pale brown, mottled with brown, yellow and grey spots, but there is a good deal of variation.

SONG Like the Herring and Lesser Black-backed Gull, the Great Black-backed Gull has the classic call *keeyow yow yow*. It also makes a slow laughing *hak hak hak* and the juveniles are frequently heard mewling indiscriminately at any adult gull.

DIET Great Black-backed Gulls are omnivorous, eating any small crustacean, fish or smaller birds, and scavenging carrion and rubbish.

HABITAT Great Black-backed Gulls are seen all around the coast, particularly in the north. Unlike the Lesser Black-backed Gull, they do not usually venture inland.

LENGTH	61–74 cm (24–29 in)
WINGSPAN	144–166 cm (57–65½ in)
BREEDING STARTS	May
NUMBER OF EGGS PER CLUTCH	2–4

Where in UK Great Black-backed Gulls can be seen

Months when Great Black-backed can be seen

OTHER These birds are savage marauders and will attack other seabirds to get them to drop their catches. They are voracious nest raiders and will take any fledgling; they have even been known to take adult Puffins and even small lambs. They are also eager scavengers and will trail fishing boats and factories to grab any discards.

COMMON TERN *Sternus hirundo*

ADULT Common Terns are bold seabirds with a striking streamlined shape and a long, sharp, forked tail. They are mostly a clean white, with pale grey wings, short red legs and black cap and black eyes. The Common Tern may be confused with the smaller Arctic Tern, but they have slightly longer legs, and a black tip to their sharp red bill. In winter the bills can be black.

JUVENILE Juveniles have brown barring on wings and back and often show partial black caps.

EGGS The Common Tern nests in mixed colonies on coastal islands or in inland wetlands. The nest is just a scrape in the ground and the eggs are a brown- or green-tinted beige with large brown and grey speckles. The fluffy brown spotted beige chicks only stay in the nest for a few days. Fed continuously by both parents, they grow quickly and can fly after 4 to 6 weeks.

SONG Terns call with a short *kic* and an ear-splitting *kyaar*.

DIET Common Terns are expert divers, looking mostly for small fish, but also taking shrimps, molluscs and insects. Common Terns usually hunt on their own or in small groups. They fly slowly over the water looking for prey, hovering briefly and then folding their wings to plunge into the water with very little splash, surfacing rapidly afterwards with any catch to be consumed at the surface.

LENGTH	34–37 cm (13½ –14½ in)
WINGSPAN	70–80 cm (28–31½ in)
BREEDING STARTS	May
NUMBER OF EGGS PER CLUTCH	2–5

Where in UK
Common Terns
can be seen

Months when
Common Terns
can be seen

J F M A M J J A S O N D

HABITAT Predominantly a coastal bird, these Terns can also be found on wetlands, reservoirs and rivers inland. They are very social and often congregate in large numbers, particularly when migrating south.

OTHER Common Terns are expert flyers and seldom swim or walk. Courting Terns engage in pair bonding, with synchronized flight, and head bobbing and beak waving when on the ground. The male often brings fish to feed the female, both before courting and afterwards. They can be very insistent and aggressive when protecting nestlings, often attacking intruders, but do not usually make actual contact.

CORMORANT *Phalacrocorax carbo*

ADULT Cormorants are large snake-necked birds with an angular head and a long bill with a pronounced hook at its tip. They appear black from a distance, but close up their feathers are a scalloped brown with a green glossy sheen. They have white cheeks, short black webbed feet, green eyes and a yellow bill with a bald yellow pouch under the lower mandible. In addition, mature adults may show a white thigh patch. They have a short square tail, used extensively as a rudder whilst swimming. They may easily be confused with the Shag, which is slightly smaller and slimmer but rarely found inland.

JUVENILE Juvenile Cormorants are paler and a duller brown in colour, with much paler underparts.

EGGS Cormorants nest in colonies, sometimes very large, building nests of twigs, seaweed and reeds perched on cliffs and in trees. The eggs are a near-perfect narrow oval shape, coloured pale blue with a chalky sheen.

SONG They employ a series of grunts and croaks in colonies, but are generally otherwise quiet.

DIET Cormorants eat live fish almost exclusively – their principle catch being small eels and flatfish. They dive for long periods, darting around underwater in pursuit of these fish.

HABITAT Cormorants are widespread and common all around the coast, but also common inland up large rivers and estuaries and on lakes and reservoirs. They are often seen in small groups but may fish alone.

OTHER Cormorants swim with head tilted up, quite low in the water, with less buoyancy than ducks and geese. They are often spotted resting between bouts of fishing, sometimes in groups, on buoys, posts or other prominent objects, pruning their feathers and spreading their wings out to dry in a characteristic upright pose. They tend to fly low and straight with rapid strong beats of their long tapering wings and with head and neck outstretched. Over flat water, they can fly very fast, skimming the surface to minimize drag.

LENGTH	77–94 cm (30–37 in)
WINGSPAN	121–149 cm (47–59 in)
BREEDING STARTS	May
NUMBER OF EGGS PER CLUTCH	3–5

Where in UK
Cormorants
can be seen

Months wh
Cormoran
can be see

J
F
M
A
M
J
J
A
S
O
N
D

COMMON SANDPIPER   *Actitis hypoleucos*

ADULT The Common Sandpiper is a medium-sized wading bird with quite a distinctive manner and colouration. Standing on short, greeny-yellow legs, it has a short neck, a long bill, and the black eye shows an obvious dark brown and white stripe. The adult has a white underside, streaky brown breast and a darker streaked-brown back and short tail, which it bobs continuously. The Common Sandpiper is easily confused with other types of Sandpiper, but unlike most of the others it does not show a white rump in flight. It has shorter legs and bill than the Red and Greenshank.

JUVENILE Juvenile Sandpipers are a more ruddy brown colour and more speckled overall.

EGGS The Sandpiper's nest is usually just a scrape in stony ground, generally hidden in low foliage. Its eggs are glossy tapered ovoids, in colour a pale blue or yellow with rusty, blue and brown speckles.

SONG The call is an insistent *twi wee wee weee*, which is quite frantic when disturbed by an intruder or when protecting chicks on the ground. Also they sometimes make just a plain *peep* to each other.

DIET Sandpipers probe the mud and shores for small crustaceans, shellfish, insects and invertebrates. They like to feed near the waterline, particularly favouring the outgoing tide.

HABITAT The Common Sandpiper is very widespread and found all along the coast and on inland wetlands, lakes and reservoirs. It is often seen in flocks, sometimes quite large, at the coast or when migrating. Inland it tends to be seen in smaller groups.

LENGTH	18–21 cm (7–8 in)
WINGSPAN	32–35 cm (12½–14 in)
BREEDING STARTS	May
NUMBER OF EGGS PER CLUTCH	4

J F M A M J J A S O N D

Where in UK Common Sandpipers can be seen

Months when Common Sandpip can be seen

OTHER In flight the Sandpiper shows dark brown, tapered wings with a white central wingbar and a short tail with white edging. The flight itself is with bursts of short, rapid, shallow wingbeats with stiff wings swept back, flying low over the water, with sharp changes in direction and often interspersed with short glides. It glides in to land delicately on its feet, bobbing gently with its tail after landing.

EIDER *Somateria mollissima*

ADULT Eider are large marine diving ducks. They are tubby and have rounded but streamlined features. The flat forehead of the large head slopes down to meet the long duckbill, forming a perfect wedge. Mature males are brightly coloured, with white upper parts and wings, a black underbelly, a black crown and tail, and half-black, tapered wings. They also have a pale green nape patch and buff or pinkish shading on the breast, and may show an obvious white thigh patch on the body when standing. The female Eider, in stark contrast, is a barred russet-brown colour all over, showing only a faint pale eye-stripe and a pair of fine white wing-bars along the wing when in flight. Both sexes have grey-black legs and large webbed feet.

JUVENILE Juvenile birds start grey-brown, the males becoming piebald as their mature plumage grows through over several years.

EGGS Eiders breed mostly on rocks and islands near to the water, lining their nests with down plucked from the female's breast. The female lays a clutch of pale green eggs, which are tucked deep into the nest on a bed of moss.

SONG Eiders coo regularly and quietly to each other, usually in triplets with the central triplet higher in pitch – *coo-oooo-oo*. There is also the occasional short *hak*, mostly from the female.

LENGTH	60–70 cm (23½–27½ in)
WINGSPAN	95–105 cm (37–41 in)
BREEDING STARTS	April
NUMBER OF EGGS PER CLUTCH	3–10

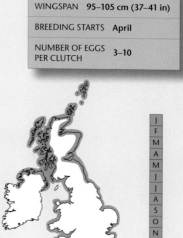

Where in UK Eider can be seen

Months when Eider can be seen

DIET Eiders feed principally on crustaceans and molluscs.

HABITAT They can be seen on the coast and out at sea, mainly in the north. Occasionally they are found inland in marshes and estuaries.

OTHER The down in the eider's nest has long been used for filling pillows and quilts. True eiderdown items are now a rarity, but harvesting continues sustainably, with down being taken after the young have left the nest.

GANNET *Morus bassanus*

ADULT Gannets are magnificent, large, streamlined seabirds. They are usually easy to identify by their exceptionally long tapering wings and distinctive colouration – a brilliant white to the elbow and black to the wingtips. The large head and long neck have a vivid yellow shading, strongest at the back. The Gannet has short black legs with large webbed feet, a short tapering tail and an impressively large, pale blue-grey dagger bill with precise black outlining. Their bright yellow eyes are enclosed in the black bill markings.

JUVENILE Juvenile Gannets start with a speckled grey-black colouration which gradually fades from head to tail and is replaced by adult plumage over several years.

EGGS Gannets nest in giant colonies on distant offshore rocky stacks. They usually lay a single large tapered ovoid egg which has a chalky covered pale blue shell. The nest is commonly a heap of seaweed and feathers.

SONG They are noisy when in their colonies, making tuneless grunts and barks, but are usually quiet out at sea.

DIET Their diet is almost exclusively live fish. They are expert flyers at low level, gliding at wing-tip height, hugging ocean waves and fish spotting, even in high winds and heavy seas. On sighting fish, Gannets usually climb then dive steeply from a height, sometimes as much as 30 m (100 ft), folding back their wings and daggering into the water at tremendous speed. Large groups of Gannets will zero in on fish shoals near the surface and 'dive bomb' the shoals repeatedly to catch fish in spectacular fashion.

LENGTH	85–97 cm (33½ –38 in)
WINGSPAN	170–192 cm (67–76 in)
BREEDING STARTS	March
NUMBER OF EGGS PER CLUTCH	1

J
F
M
A
M
J
J
A
S
O
N
D

Where in UK Gannets can be seen

Months when Gannets can be seen

HABITAT Gannets are spotted out at sea all round the coast. They are rarely seen close to the shore of the mainland, but are common around islands.

OTHER Gannets are masters of their element. They are constantly on the move, setting out on fishing trips or wheeling round the colony. They are highly social birds with complex courting displays of mutual pointing and bowing.

RAZORBILL *Alca torda*

ADULT The Razorbill is so named because of its heavy, blunt-looking hooked bill, which is very strong and sharp. They are tubby streamlined seabirds, smartly coloured with pitch black above and a brilliant white below. The bill is black and has a fine, neat white stripe running over the tips of the upper and lower mandible and along the upper to meet the black eye. In winter, this line is often less distinct and the throat and breast change to white. The Razorbill can be confused with the Guillemot, but is stockier, with a pointy tail and blunt bill.

JUVENILE Juvenile birds are coloured much the same as adults, but they may be slightly duller and browner.

EGGS The Razorbill lays a single narrow oval-shaped egg, rough textured and pale tinted brown or green with variable brown speckles. The nest is just a depression on a ledge on a rocky cliff or offshore sea stack.

SONG They are generally very quiet birds, but occasionally emit a series of groans and rapid croaks to each other.

DIET Razorbills feed mainly by diving for shellfish.

HABITAT These birds are mostly seen out at sea or around cliffs and rocky islands, although sometimes they will dive around harbours and pilings. They are more common in the north of the country, where they breed

LENGTH	39–43 cm (15–17 in)
WINGSPAN	60–69 cm (23½–27 in)
BREEDING STARTS	May
NUMBER OF EGGS PER CLUTCH	1

Where in UK Razorbills can be seen

Months when Razorbills can be seen

Adult

Juvenile

OTHER Razorbills are gregarious birds, living in large remotely located colonies and often seen hunting together in groups, sometimes mixed with Guillemots. They fly straight and direct with rapid beats of their narrow wings, and with their short black legs and large webbed feet tucked out of view under their short pointy tail. They are completely at home in heavy seas, riding out the swell, frequently clustered together in groups. Razorbills will frequently employ an extended take-off from the water, running along the surface while flapping rapidly to gain height. On land they are ungainly, standing upright, but waddling around quite clumsily.

PUFFIN *Fratercula arctica*

ADULT Puffins are small, comical-looking, tubby, black and white seabirds. Both the male and the female have striking large triangular bills that are brightly coloured blue and red with yellow outlining. To complement the bill, they have a clown-like white face patch on either side of their black heads with a triangular black patch and stripe from the eye. The eye is black with a fine red rim. In winter, the face goes greyer and the bill is duller.

JUVENILES Juveniles are like the winter adult, but gain adult plumage after just a single year.

EGGS The male Puffin builds the nest, digging a tunnel into soft soil, and lining it with grass, leaves and feathers. Sometimes Puffins will make use of old Manx Shearwater or rabbit burrows and, where the ground is too hard, they nest under boulders or in cracks and cavities in cliffs. The eggs are creamy white, occasionally tinged with lilac. Both parents incubate the egg and feed the chick.

SONG Puffins are quite noisy, constantly emitting a quiet *arr*.

DIET Puffins eat fish, especially sand eel, and herring. They can hold several small fish at a time, crosswise in their bill. This allows them to carrry more food for their chick than a bird that can only carry one fish at a time.

HABITAT Colonies of Puffins nest on remote islands and offshore stacks. After breeding, they winter at sea, usually far from the coast.

OTHER Puffins can 'fly' almost as well underwater as they can in the air. Airborne, they fly very directly with rapid beats of their short straight wings, and use their large orange webbed feet and small black tail to brake when landing.

LENGTH:	**32 cm (12½ in)**
WINGSPAN:	**53 cm (21 in)**
BREEDING STARTS	**Late April**
NUMBER OF EGGS PER CLUTCH	1

Where in UK
Puffins
can be seen

Months when
Puffins
can be seen

COMMON GUILLEMOT   *Uria aalge*

ADULT   The Common Guillemot is a long, sleek but tubby bird, coloured very dark brown, looking almost black on top and brilliant white underneath. During the winter the white extends from the breast to the birds face, leaving a black collar and revealing a black line extending behind the eye. During the summer the face turns black and may have a thin white border to the black eye, with a fine white line running behind the eye. Guillemots have a long and narrow black dagger bill, very short black legs and webbed feet. Common Guillemots can be confused with the Black Guillemot and the Razorbill, which are of similar size and colour, although Black Guillemots have bright red legs and feet and Razorbills have a heavy blunter bill.

JUVENILE   Juveniles are similarly coloured, but slightly paler.

EGGS   The Guillemot nests on rocky crags, cliffs and offshore stacks packed close together in large colonies. It lays a single heavily tapered egg that is a variable dull pale tint with fine dark speckles. When incubating, the adult will balance the egg on its feet under its breast to keep it warm.

SONG   Guillemots have a repetitive laughing *ha ha ha* in colonies, particularly when defending nesting sites, and also grunt and groan to each other.

LENGTH	38–46 cm (15–18 in)
WINGSPAN	61–73 cm (24–29 in)
BREEDING STARTS	April
NUMBER OF EGGS PER CLUTCH	1

Where in UK Common Guillemots can be seen

Months when Common Guillem... can be seen

DIET   Guillemots dive from the surface to catch fish and squid. They are exceptionally good swimmers underwater, 'flying' in much the same way as they do above the surface.

HABITAT   Found only around the coast and out at sea, they are frequently seen swimming in the water and diving to chase fish. Occasionally they are seen sheltering along the coasts when the weather is very bad at sea.

OTHER   In flight the Guillemot tends to fly low and straight with very rapid wingbeats – their feet extend beyond their very short tail. Guillemots are clumsy on land, standing upright and waddling around on their large webbed feet. They are very sociable birds, often seen in small flocks and they have a pairing display of mutual bowing and head waving.

HERRING GULL   *Larus argentatus*

ADULT   The Herring Gull is a large aggressive gull, coloured like the Common Gull, with a clean white head, neck and underparts, with grey wings and back. It has black wingtips with white spots or 'mirrors', pale pink legs, and a bright yellow bill with a red spot on the lower bill. The young chicks in the nest peck at the bill spot to encourage the adult to regurgitate food. The Herring Gull is easily confused with the Common Gull (which is much smaller) and immature Lesser and Greater Black-backed Gulls (it can be difficult to distinguish the Herring Gull from these).

JUVENILE   The Juvenile gull shows a speckled brown tail and back, with a black tail band and lightly speckled underparts. Wings have brown speckles with very dark primary feathers.

EGGS   The Herring Gull commonly nests in large colonies on steep and rocky ground or islands. Its nest is usually dry grass and may be used year after year. The eggs are variable in colour, usually olive or pale brown with dark brown and grey speckles and streaks.

SONG   The Herring Gull and the Black-backed Gulls are the only seagulls with the classic call: *keeyow yow yow*. Both commonly throw back their heads and let loose this piercing cry. The Herring Gull also makes an insistent *kah kah kah* and the juveniles are frequently to be heard mewling at the parents, even when fully grown.

DIET   Herring Gulls are always on the lookout for easy pickings but, despite their name, they don't eat herring by preference – though they will eat just about anything else. They are habitual bullies and will hound smaller seabirds to drop their catches; they rob nests, and frequently catch young birds and mammals.

LENGTH	54–60 cm (21–24 in)
WINGSPAN	123–148 cm (48–58 in)
BREEDING STARTS	March
NUMBER OF EGGS PER CLUTCH	2–4

J F M A M J J A S O N D

Where in UK Herring Gulls can be seen

Months when Herring Gulls can be seen

HABITAT   Mostly seen around coastlines or near large rivers, they also favour reservoirs, rubbish tips and sewage works. Herring Gulls can often be seen soaring at height in groups.

OTHER   These birds are quick learners and adopt a variety of ingenious ways to gain food. Methods such as dropping shellfish and crabs from heights onto rocks to smash them, or tapping on windows to 'ask' humans for food are commonplace. Herring Gulls are long lived and numerous and have become a common nuisance in seaside towns.

KITTIWAKE   *Rissa tridactyla*

ADULT   Kittiwakes are medium-sized and have a less aggressive-looking face than other gulls. Both sexes are mostly white and have a small head with black eyes, and a yellow beak with a bright red gape. They have short black legs and black wing tips. The wings are pale grey above with fine white trailing edges. In winter, adults may show a black ear patch that is more common on juveniles. Kittiwakes can be confused with the slightly smaller Common Gull, but Kittiwakes have shorter legs and no spots or 'mirrors' on the wing.

JUVENILE   Juvenile Kittiwakes have a black collar round the back of the neck, a black ear spot, black tail bar, and a strong black leading edge to the wing joining up the black wingtips. This can show as a strong black W across the upper wings whilst in flight.

EGGS   Kittiwakes nest in huge colonies consisting of many thousands of birds, packed onto ledges on vertiginous cliffs. Nests are made on rock ledges on these cliffs, and lined with seaweed and moss. The eggs are large tapered ovoids, a matt cream or tinted colour with grey, purple, yellow and brown speckles.

SONG   This bird is named after its repetitive call, *ke-ke-week*, which ends on a high-pitched *week*. Colonies are a constant cacophony of cries as birds call to each other and any intruders, but when they are away from the colony the birds are mostly quiet.

DIET   Kittiwakes live on small fish, crustaceans, molluscs and squid, but are happy to scavenge discards from coastal fisheries and boats.

HABITAT   Found only along sea coasts and out at sea, Kittiwakes are rarely seen inland. They like to glide quietly along sea coasts and out at sea, looking for easy pickings and fishing boat discards.

| LENGTH   37–42 cm (14½ –16½ in) |
| WINGSPAN   93–105 cm (36½ –41 in) |
| BREEDING STARTS   **May** |
| NUMBER OF EGGS PER CLUTCH   **2–3** |

Where in UK
Kittiwakes
can be seen

Months when
Kittiwakes
can be seen

OTHER   Kittiwake colonies usually smell very strongly of fishy guano. These colonies can be found in the Pacific, southeast Alaska, in the Atlantic, Greenland as well as the high Arctic islands.

OYSTERCATCHER *Haematopus ostralegus*

ADULT Oystercatchers are smart black and white birds standing tall on long bright pink legs. They have a distinctive long, straight, bright orange bill, which they use to probe sand and mud in search of shellfish and worms. The bird is mostly black on top with a black head and a red eye, ringed in red. Their all-white underparts and breast show forward of the folded wing from the side view, but the head and neck is completely black. In flight they show a white rump, a white band along their tapering wings and a black tail bar on their relatively short tails. From underneath the wings show completely white apart from a strong black trailing edge.

JUVENILE Juvenile birds are coloured much the same as adults, but they may be slightly duller and browner, and have a white throat collar plus a duller bill with darkened tip.

EGGS Oystercatcher eggs are beige-speckled with dark spots, splotches and streaks, laid on the ground in just a scrape in sand or shingle, with little or no nesting material.

SONG The Oystercatcher is habitually noisy, emitting a piping *kip kip* which often accelerates, becoming a desperately shrill *kleep kleep kleep* when the bird is disturbed or protecting young on the ground.

DIET Oystercatchers feed on marine worms, shrimps, small crabs and a variety of shellfish such as cockles, mussels and limpets. Inland they will forage for insects and earthworms. Their bills are ideal implements for prising open shellfish or hammering holes through hard shells.

LENGTH	39–44 cm (15–17 in)
WINGSPAN	72–83 cm (28–33 in)
BREEDING STARTS	April
NUMBER OF EGGS PER CLUTCH	2–4

J F M A M J J A S O N D

| Where in UK Oystercatchers can be seen | Months when Oystercatchers can be seen |

HABITAT Oystercatchers are easily spotted around the coasts and up estuaries; they will nest inland, particularly in the north.

OTHER They are quite sociable birds, often feeding in groups on sandy or muddy shores and gathering together when roosting, sometimes in large flocks. Pairs tend to be faithful to each other and their nesting place, with one pair defending the same site for 20 years.

FULMAR *Fulmarus glacialis*

ADULT Fulmars have the appearance of short stocky seagulls. They have a thick-set white head, white underparts and grey shading over the back and upper wings, darkening towards the wingtips. The short tail is grey and often fanned out when flying. There are no black markings, as on most seagulls, but they do have black eyes. Their very short grey legs and feet mean they are only able to walk very awkwardly on the ground. There is some variation in birds from different regions, with darker birds from the north and Arctic. The yellow beak of the Fulmar is short, heavy and blocky and has a prominent grey tubular nostril on the top. Fulmars are not strictly speaking seagulls, but are part of the family of Petrels who share this feature.

JUVENILE Juvenile Fulmars look very similar to the adults in colouration, but may appear a little duller and less distinct.

EGGS The Fulmar nests in colonies on vertiginous cliffs and rock stacks. It lays a single large symmetrical egg that is a plain creamy white colour with a fine dusting of rusty spots. This is generally laid into a depression on a bare rocky ledge.

SONG The voice is mainly just cackles and moans amongst each other in colonies. Courting couples wave their heads with bills open while busily cackling at each other.

LENGTH	42–50 cm (16½–19½ in)
WINGSPAN	100–118 cm (39–46½in)
BREEDING STARTS	May
NUMBER OF EGGS PER CLUTCH	1

J
F
M
A
M
J
J
A
S
O
N
D

Where in UK
Fulmars
can be seen

Months when
Fulmars
can be seen

DIET Fulmars live mainly on a diet of crustaceans and fish, but are very keen on scavenging from the sea surface.

HABITAT They are widespread but generally only seen out at sea and along coastlines, mainly near rocky cliffs and offshore islands.

OTHER Fulmars are often seen gliding low over open ocean waves, even in high seas, or along vertical cliff sides. They glide effortlessly with wings stiffly outstretched, banking steeply on their wingtips to change direction. Both the adults and the chicks are able to defend themselves with an accurately aimed noxious mix of regurgitated stomach contents and gastric juices.

SHAG *Phalacrocorax aristotelis*

ADULT Adult Shags, like Cormorants, are large snake-necked birds with an angular head and a long bill with a pronounced hook at its tip. Shags are almost completely black with a scalloped, glossy, green sheen to the feathers. They have short black webbed feet, green eyes and a yellow bill with a bald yellow pouch under the lower mandible. In addition, mature adults may show a black crest, which can make the head look quite square from a distance. They have a short square tail, used extensively as a rudder whilst swimming. Shags are slightly smaller and slimmer than the Cormorant, with which they are often confused. They tend to fly with their necks straighter than Cormorants, and appear to have a blockier head.

JUVENILE Juvenile Shags are paler dull brown in colour, with much paler underparts fading to white under the chin (but not as pale as juvenile Cormorants). The bill may be pale or grey-brown to black.

EGGS Shags nest in colonies, which may be very large, on inaccessible cliffs and sea stacks. They build nests of sticks, seaweed and grass. The eggs are a narrow oval shape, pale blue and with a chalky sheen.

SONG They are noisy birds, croaking and hissing when in their colonies. They are usually quiet, though, out at sea.

LENGTH	68–80 cm (26.8–31.5 in)
WINGSPAN	95–110 cm (37.4–43.3 in)
BREEDING STARTS	February
NUMBER OF EGGS PER CLUTCH	3-4

J
F
M
A
M
J
J
A
S
O
N
D

Where in UK
Shags
can be seen

Months when
Shags
can be seen

DIET The diet is almost exclusively live fish, principally sand-eels and flatfish.

HABITAT Shags are only found on the coast and out at sea, rarely inland. They may be seen in small groups or fishing alone.

OTHER Shags fly fast, low and direct over the sea with rapid strong beats of their long, tapering wings. Inflight their head and neck are stretched out straight. They have similar habits to their larger cousin, the Cormorant, swimming with head tilted up and sitting quite low in the water. They dive for long periods in pursuit of fish. They are often spotted resting between bouts of fishing, sometimes in groups on buoys or rocky knolls, pruning their feathers and holding their wings out to dry in a characteristic upright pose.

LESS COMMON BIRDS

GREAT SKUA   *Catharacta skua*

The Great Skua is the largest in a group of gull-like seabirds. Looking much like a juvenile Black-backed Gull, it is heavy-set, with a large, slightly hooked, brown-black bill. These Skuas are coloured a dark speckled brown all over and show white patches on the wings when in flight. Juvenile Skuas are similarly coloured, but with plainer brown undersides.

Skuas are master plunderers which attack other seabirds to make them release or regurgitate their catch. They also plunder other seabirds' nests and will take fledglings and occasionally even adult puffins. Found mainly out at sea, they breed mostly in the northern isles. They are renowned for their aggressive protection of their nesting sites, attacking any intruder relentlessly.

Razorbills are gregarious birds, living in large remotely located colonies and often seen hunting together in groups, sometimes mixed with Guillemots. They fly straight and direct with rapid beats of their narrow wings, and with their short black legs and large webbed feet tucked out of view under their short pointy tail. They are completely at home in heavy seas, riding out the swell, frequently clustered together in groups. Razorbills will frequently employ an extended take-off from the water, running along the surface while flapping rapidly to gain height. On land they are ungainly, standing upright, but waddling around quite clumsily.

ROCK CHOUGH *Pyrrhocorax pyrrhocorax*

The Rock Chough, generally found in fields on the rocky coasts of
Cornwall and Wales, is at first glance just another large Crow
with glossy black plumage and fingered wingtips. However,
it has a long, bright red down-curved bill and red legs.
The juvenile Chough is similarly coloured with a
yellowy bill, but it is duller overall.

These are highly sociable, playful flyers and seem
to enjoy wheeling around in the wind over cliffs,
rolling and diving together in small groups, while
whistling a cheerful musical *keeaw*. Like many
other crows, Rock Choughs pick over areas of
grass for small insects and invertebrates. They
nest high up on cliff sides and on rocky outcrops.

STORM PETREL *Hydrobates pelagicus*

Storm Petrels are from a family of tiny black seabirds and resemble
swallows. The adult shows a brilliant white rump and
underside wing bar, but has a short, rounded tail with
no fork. They fly with swept-back wings and dangling
legs, flitting over the surface of the water with feet
trailing on the surface, as they take small shrimp
and fish in their short black bill.

Petrels often follow in the wake of ships. They
spend all their time in the open sea, only being
seen inland or on the coast as a result of extreme
storms and winds. They land only on remote sea
stacks and islands to breed in burrows.

BIRDS OF PREY

MERLIN *Falco columbarius*

Compact of size and dashing of flight, the Merlin is the UK's smallest bird of prey, not much bigger than a Blackbird. Identified by its long, squared tail and broad-based wings, the Merlin flies with rapid wing beats, occasionally gliding.

Because of its size (the bird weighs only four ounces) it easily hovers over prey before taking it in mid-air – sometimes the Merlin will even bring down quarry larger than itself. In the breeding season the male will fly with its catch towards the nest while calling, then stop at a 'plucking post' to decapitate the quarry before either taking the body to the female or calling her to pass the body mid-air.

EGGS Lays between May and June; both parents incubate and tend to nestlings

SONG Rapid *quik-ik-ik-ik-ik*. Usually a male calling to his mate when he has food

DIET Small birds, mammals and lizards; occasionally insects and game chicks

HABITAT During the breeding season, from April to October, found in upland moorland areas. Migrates south to inland lowland and coastal areas during winter. Will roost in reed beds, bogs and heaths, often with Hen Harriers

PEREGRINE *Falco peregrinus*

A large, powerful falcon, the Peregrine has long, broad, pointed wings and a relatively short tail. In flight it is a most spectacular hunter. Soaring high above its hunting ground, the Peregrine spots its prey and arches through the sky in a dive or stoop that can reach speeds of up to 290 km (180 miles) per hour. If the bird misses, it will continue to stoop at its prey until successful. The talons can hit with such force that when killing a bird mid-air it has been known for the quarry zIn the past, Peregrines have been persecuted, although the number of breeding pairs now stands at almost 1,500. During the SecondWorld War large numbers were shot as it was thought they were a threat to the Carrier Pigeons used when radio silence was imposed on submarine-spotting planes.

EGGS Three or four eggs laid around April and incubated for 28 days, mainly by the female

SONG Elongated *kweeee-kweeee-kweeeee-kweeee*

DIET Medium-sized birds, killed on the wing; sometimes rabbits and small mammals

HABITAT During the breeding season, can be found along rocky sea cliffs and upland areas; in winter, they congregate in east coast marshland

WHITE-TAILED EAGLE *Haliaeetus albicilla*

The White-tailed Eagle is the largest of the country's birds of prey. It is identified by brown body plumage and conspicuously paler head and neck, which in older birds can become white, and a white tail.

This magnificent bird was extinct by the early nineteenth century as a result of birds being killed illegally. Thanks to a breeding programme, which saw 82 young Norwegian eagles being released on the island of Rhum between 1975 and 1985, the population is now self-sustaining.

EGGS Two or three eggs laid 2–3 days apart in March or April, incubated by the female

SONG Almost a clucking cry

DIET Largely fish, but will also take birds, rabbits and hares. Opportunistic White-tailed Eagles will take carrion and pirate food from other animals such as otters

HABITAT Outer Hebrides and west coast of Scotland; slowly being reintroduced to the east coast of Scotland

The photographic images listed below are specifically licensed by the photographers for use in this publication, and are subject to copyright.

Nigel Blake
Barn Owl p.105, Black-headed Gull p.187, Blackcap p.65, Brambling p.71, Bullfinch p.72, Buzzard p.142, Chaffinch p.35, Coal Tit pp.3 and 77, Collared Dove p.36, Common Gull p.189, Common Sandpiper p.197, Common Tern p.192, Cuckoo p.100, Curlew p.155, Dipper p.111, Dotterel p.141, Dunlin p.20, Dunnock p.65, Fieldfare p.113, Goldcrest p.23, Golden Plover p.121, Great Black-backed Gull p.191, Great Cormorant p.195, Great Crested Grebe p.157, Greater Spotted Woodpecker p.2, Greenfinch p.41, Grey Partridge p.115, House Martin p.45, Jay p.85, Kestrel p.102, Kingfisher p.161, Lapwing p.163, Linnet p.119, Little Owl p.104, Long-tailed Tit p.87, Mistle Thrush p.88, Nightingale pp.10 and 100, Nuthatch pp.68 and 91, Pied Wagtail p.127, Red Grouse p.117, Red Kite p.6, Redshank p.173, Skylark p.109, Spotted Flycatcher p.79, Starling p.55, Stock Dove p.92, Stonechat p.133, Tawny Owl p.104, Teal p.177, Treecreeper p.95, Water Rail p.169, Wheatear pp.8 and 137, Whinchat p.139, Wren p.60, Yellow Wagtail p.131

Bruce Winslade
Arctic Tern pp.24 and 185, Barnacle Goose p.149, Blackbird pp.11 and 31, Blue Tit p.33, Carrion Crow p.39, Coot pp.14, 147 and 153, Eider Duck pp19 and 198, Fulmar p.215, Gannet p.201, Goldfinch p.65, Greylag Goose p.144, Great Tit p.42, Grey Heron p.158, Guillemot p.207, Herring Gull p.209, House Sparrow pp.16, 46 and 63, Jackdaw p.64, Kittiwake p.210, Little Egret p.178, Mallard p.165, Moorhen p.167, Mute Swan p.175, Oystercatcher p.213, Peregrine Falcon p.220, Pintail p.179, Puffin p.204, Raven p.140, Razorbill p.203, Ringed Plover p.178, Robin pp.1 and 50, Rook pp13 and 125, Shag p.217, Shelduck p.171, Snow Bunting p.141, Song Thrush p.53, Sparrowhawk p.103, Wood Pigeon pp.66 and 97

Steve Round
Common Swift p.22, Great Skua p.218, Marsh Harrier p.180, Twite p.135, Wood Warbler p.99

Peter Gray
Curlew p.106, Great Skua p.218, White-tailed Eagle pp.18 and 221

Sue Tranter
Barn Swallow p.57, Tree Pipit p.101

Jerzyk Tabor
Common Swift p.59

Jan Bosch
Montagu's Harrier p.181

The photographic images listed below are licensed under Creative Commons licences; copyright remains with the photographer.

Aleph
Chiffchaff p.75
Andreas Trepte
Brent Goose p.151
Ring Ouzel p.123
Andrei Stroe
Green Woodpecker p.81
Andrzej Jabłecki
Hawfinch p.83
Chuck Abbe
Golden Eagle p.142
Dean Morley
Avocet p.178
Ernst Vikne
Siskin p.64
Lily M.
Eurasian Hobby p.102
Malte Uhl
Rock Chough p.219
Martien Brand
Little Grebe p.179
Mike Baird
Osprey p.181
David Iliff
Skylark p.129

Norbert Kenner
Goshawk p.103
Otter
Storm Petrel p.219
Per Harald Olsen
Rock Ptarmigan p.140
Marek Slusarczyk
Rock Ptarmigan p.140
Pete Birkinshaw
Magpie pp.12 and 49
Raj Boora
Merlin p.220
Sascha Rösner
Long-eared Owl p.105
Stevie B
Barn Owl p.17
Terry Ross
Osprey p.181
Thermos
Lesser Spotted Woodpecker p.101
Thomas Kraft
Red Kite p.143
Tony Hisgett
Common Pochard p.179

Bird illustration sources

H. E. Dresser, from *Birds of Britain*, 1907
Blackbird p.30, Black-headed Gull p.186, Chiffchaff p.74, Great Black-backed Gull p.190, Great Tit p.42, Herring Gull p.208, Kittiwake p.210, Mallard p.164, Moorhen p.166, Oystercatcher p.212, Razorbill p.202, Robin p.50, Rook p.124, Shag p.216, Shelduck p.170, Song Thrush p.52, Chaffinch p.34, Curlew p.154, Fieldfare p.112, Great Crested Grebe p.156, Greenfinch p.40, Grey Partridge p.114, Jay p.84, Kingfisher p.160, Lapwing p.162, Long-tailed Tit p.86, Pied Wagtail p.126, Red Grouse p.116, Redshank p.172, Ring Ouzel p.122, Spotted Flycatcher p.78, Starling p.54, Stonechat p.132, Common Tern p.192, Treecreeper p.94, Water Rail p.168, Wheatear p.136, Wren p.60, Nuthatch p.90, Magpie p.48, Common Swift p.58

John Gould, from *The Birds of Europe*, Wood Pigeon p.66

Johann Friedrich Naumann, from *Naturgeschichte der Vögel Mitteleuropas* and other publications
Brent Goose p.150, Green Woodpecker p.80, Hawfinch p.82, Barnacle Goose p.148, Blue Tit p.32, Coot p.152, Eider p.19, 198, Fulmar p.214, Gannet p.200, Grey Heron p.158, Mute Swan p.174, Puffin p.204, Carrion Crow p.38, Coal Tit p.76, Sandpiper p.196, Teal p.176, Cormorant p.194, Dipper p.110, House Martin p.44, Mistle Thrush p.88, Yellow Wagtail p.130, Whinchat p.138, Wood Warbler p.98, Barn Swallow p.56, Hooded Crow p.38

Magnus, Ferdinand and Wilhelm von Wright, from *Svenska fåglar, efter naturen och på sten ritade*
Guillemot p.206, House Sparrow p.46, Brambling p.70, Bullfinch p.72, Golden Plover p.120, Linnet p.118, Stock Dove p.92, Skylark p.128, Twite p.134